From the Edge of the Ghetto

African Americans and the World of Work

Alford A. Young, Jr.
University of Michigan

ROWMAN & LITTLEFIELD
Lanham • Boulder • New York • London

Executive Editor: Rolf Janke
Assistant Editor: Courtney Packard
Senior Marketing Manager: Amy Whitaker

Credits and acknowledgments for material borrowed from other sources, and reproduced with permission, appear on the appropriate page within the text.

Published by Rowman & Littlefield
An imprint of The Rowman & Littlefield Publishing Group, Inc.
4501 Forbes Boulevard, Suite 200, Lanham, Maryland 20706
https://rowman.com

6 Tinworth Street, London SE11 5AL, United Kingdom

British Library Cataloguing in Publication Information Available

Library of Congress Cataloging-in-Publication Data Available

Library of Congress Control Number: 2019949870

ISBN 9780742570092 (cloth) | ISBN 9780742570108 (pbk.) |
   ISBN 9780742570115 (electronic)

For Alford III and Kai,

who went from boys to the edge of manhood during this time

Contents

Acknowledgments

From the Edge of the Ghetto was a labor of love. The work was produced out of my deep, personal interest in a small city that I desperately needed to get to know in order to find comfort and security as an African American living in Ann Arbor, Michigan. As such, a strong blend of personal and scholarly purpose fueled this effort. I am humbled by the willingness of many African Americans in Ypsilanti to share so much of themselves—their hopes, dreams, insecurities, and perplexities—with my research team and me.

Sheldon Danziger and the National Poverty Center at the Gerald R. Ford School of Public Policy (at the University of Michigan) supported this endeavor financially, intellectually, and emotionally. It would not have happened without his commitments on each front. I am immensely grateful to him.

I am also grateful for the Association of Black Sociologists, at whose annual meeting in 2005 the initial ideas for this book were presented. Other scholarly gatherings where I shared ideas and content include the Urban Sociology Workshop in the Department of Sociology and the Center for the Ethnography of Everyday Life at the Institute for Social Research, both at the University of Michigan.

Three people deserve special acknowledgment for their role in getting my research team and me access to the men and women in this book. The first is the late Joan Chesler, who provided me with my first exposure to social service organizations in Ypsilanti. The second is Marty Moss, owner of Rammos barbershop, who provided me with access to some of the first people whom I talked to in this city. The third is Anthony Williamson, who brought me into parts of Ypsilanti that I never knew I would or could encounter and who was responsible for my connecting with the lion's share of the people in this book.

A slew of University of Michigan students and summer research program participants assisted in interviewing, coding, and analysis. They include Kristal Hall, Tynisa Compton, Jessica Welburn, Angela Veitch, Derrick Bryan, Otonye Amadi, Sabrina Charles, George Carter III, Alfred

Defreece, Trevor Gardner, Kareem Johnson, Robyn Kent, Shawn Christian, Maria Johnson, LeiLani Vance, Darion Blalock, Christina Phelps, and Matthew Alemu (who provided more time on task with this endeavor than anyone). The transcription of interviews was performed quite admirably by Jennifer Cox.

Critical readings of this material were conducted by Matthew Alemu, Aunrika Tucker-Shabazz, Luke Schaefer, Cavar Reid, Larry Root, Jeffrey Morenoff, Lydia Wiledan, Tom Fricke, and Elizabeth Rudd. Earl Lewis not only read the work but gave me a clearer sense of purpose and definition for it than I had prior to his encountering it.

Several individuals at Rowman & Littlefield were central in transforming a research project into a monograph. The late Alan McClare presented me with a contract. He was the first who saw this work as being worthy of publication, and he launched that possibility. Sarah Stanton, who assumed Alan's duties upon his passing and is now formerly of Rowman & Littlefield, demonstrated unbelievable patience and support. I am not sure that she continued to believe that this book would ever be completed, but she never wavered in supporting my efforts to do so. The third is Rolf Janke, who stepped in at Rowman & Littlefield as Sarah stepped away and saw the project to its completion. Rolf, you served as the anchor for this superb relay team of editors. Others at Rowman & Littlefield who contributed to this effort include Jehanne Schweitzer, Courtney Packard, and Sharon Langworthy.

My deepest gratitude goes to Sandra Smith, who was my partner in crime in securing a site for this project and in conducting some of the interviews. What ultimately mattered more than her involvement in the fieldwork was her involvement in shaping my intellectual vision. She was a consistent and sharp critic who helped me to be clear about asking the right questions and making the right interpretations of the responses they garnered. Every conversation with her made me a better scholar and this a better book.

Finally, my partner in life, Carla O'Connor, serves as the only person in the world who shares in my professional life as my colleague and in my personal life as my spouse. To have her commit to such double duty is a remarkable act of courage on her part. She played a role in every phase of this project, from conception to completion. Whatever scholarly capabilities that I have been fortunate to acquire in my life are secondary to the luck that I have maintained in having her in it.

Introduction

From the Edge of the Ghetto unearths the thoughts and perspectives about work and work opportunity held by 103 low-income African Americans who reside in Ypsilanti, Michigan (population about 20,000). Located about 30 miles west of Detroit, Ypsilanti is a 4.5-square-mile town that does not appear on the radar screen of many people. It is also on the eastern doorstep of Ann Arbor, a city that is home to one of America's most highly regarded public universities, the University of Michigan, and a place that for some time has been considered one of the most livable small cities in America.[1] Ypsilanti has no such public image.

As a site for automobile manufacturing, Ypsilanti is a city that bloomed during America's twentieth-century industrial boom. It did so along with much of the rest of southeastern Michigan and that region's anchor city of Detroit. The recent flourishing of postindustrialism, exemplified by the rise of technology and the kinds of specialized knowledge that have proliferated in many university and college towns, has not benefited Ypsilanti as much as it has Ann Arbor. Thus, many of Ypsilanti's residents, including many of its African Americans, live in a small city reflecting the demise of industrialism even as they also reside on the border of a model of postindustrial success.

Graduate students from the University of Michigan often can find more affordable housing in Ypsilanti. The same holds true for the employees of that university who have lower-tier jobs or others of various socioeconomic classes who simply want more for their money than what can be found in Ann Arbor. Indeed, some pockets of western Ypsilanti might seem to be indistinguishable from parts of Ann Arbor. Accordingly, Ypsilanti has residential spaces of privilege and stability, yet it also has a constituency of struggling African Americans. That constituency is visible to those who frequent the city but perhaps is never much thought about by those who have little reason to be there. Many of Ypsilanti's most economically challenged African Americans live in its southwestern, southern, eastern, and northeastern sections. Given its small size, these parts of the city are quite visible to those living in Ypsilanti. How-

1

ever, they are not easily noticed by people who move between Ann Arbor and the greater Detroit region, especially Detroit's most economically vibrant western suburbs. Consequently, Ypsilanti is one of thousands of small American cities that are not just unfamiliar but largely irrelevant to people who think of modern-day African Americans as large-city people and of the African American experience as distinctively urban.

The association of large cities with the African American poor is a twentieth-century phenomenon (Grossman 1991; Hine, Hine, and Harrold 2012; Hunter and Robinson 2016; Kusmer and Trotter 2009; Lemann 1991; Marks 1988; Tolnay 2003; Trotter 1991). In the decades following World War II, scholars and policy analysts began to consider the urban sphere as a site of immense challenge and concern for low-income people, especially African Americans. Discussions about race and urban poverty focused on America's largest cities: New York City, Chicago, and Los Angeles, as well Atlanta, Detroit, Washington, DC, and St. Louis. Those most knowledgeable about African American poverty understand that these cities, together with Houston and San Francisco, housed the lion's share of African American urban poverty in the decades following World War II (Wilson 1987). More important, urban poverty researchers have documented how the extreme concentration of such folks in selected urban geographic areas and neighborhoods fueled the vast array of conditions and problems that constitute the crisis of African American poverty (Jargowsky 1997; Jargowsky and Bane 1991; Massey and Denton 1993; Wilson 1987). Telling the story of what it means to be African American and impoverished, then, usually means telling a story about life experiences and conditions in one of these rather large places.

When considering the situations of economically disadvantaged African Americans in smaller cities, places that come to mind to those knowledgeable about that condition include Camden, New Jersey; Gary, Indiana; and East St. Louis, Illinois (Barnes 2005; Hamer 2001; Gauen 2012; Gillette 2005; Moore 2006; Editorial Board 2012; Simon 2012; Yamiche 2013; Zernicke 2014).[2] By the end of the twentieth century, all of these small cities had become notorious hotbeds of crime and social malaise. Ypsilanti is not a large city with wide and vast pockets of African American poverty, nor is it a small city with a widespread public image problem for its lower-income African American residents. There are no large-scale blighted neighborhoods (often pejoratively called ghettoes) in Ypsilanti. Instead, there are small sections of the city, wholly avoidable to those who may pass through Ypsilanti on the interstate highway, where many of the city's socioeconomically disadvantaged African Americans are housed.

That being said, one may wonder, "Why Ypsilanti? Why invest in the views of work and work opportunity held by struggling African Americans in a town that barely registers to people outside of southeastern Michigan? Why devote so much attention to this agenda when the contemporary national conversation about socioeconomically disadvantaged African Americans has largely—and perhaps necessarily—focused on the largest cities in America?"

The answer is that Ypsilanti matters because it offers a particular case of how low-income African Americans struggle to survive in what was once a thriving, single-industry small city. Ypsilanti is an American city that was a site of possibility and promise due to its location amid a thriving automobile industry. It was once upon a time a symbol of the success of industrial America due to the proliferation of automobile manufacturing plants both there and in the surrounding southeastern Michigan region. It is now a small city many of whose residents, including many of its 9,000 African American residents, are in search of a secure place in America's future and do not easily find it in the contemporary, postindustrial period. This being the case, *From the Edge of the Ghetto* offers a testimony that Ypsilanti is an important place to think about when trying to make sense of the contemporary experiences of African Americans in disadvantage.

In a small single-industry city like Ypsilanti, hope for black Americans meant the chance to immerse oneself in the automobile manufacturing sector, an employment arena that decades ago engineered opportunity in this town. Accordingly, for these residents hope for a better future is tied to how much that occupational sector has shaped their images and understandings of the desirable and the possible concerning work and work opportunity, as well as of what is neither desirable nor comprehensible to them as they strive to make sense of the modern world of work. Furthermore, as the following pages illustrate, African Americans in small cities often experience different kinds of contact with and exposure to people of greater privilege than do those in large cities.

Rather than privilege being associated with faraway or inaccessible places, Ypsilanti's proximity to Ann Arbor places privilege on the geographic doorstep of those living amid poverty in that small city. Small-city African Americans who reside near places of privilege are physically situated to think about space in ways that are distinct from the large-city experience. This is because those in the small city are not encumbered by the geographic isolation that comes with living in so-called urban ghettoes. Instead, often only a few blocks in either direction from their residences constitute their notion of the *hood*. Yet for black Ypsilantians (as I refer to them in this book) the big city, in this case Detroit, remains central in their conversations about what they consider to be meaningful work for people like themselves. This is because the Detroit story of automobile manufacturing as providing great financial return to people who did not go to college or seek places in a white-collar professional world also infiltrates black Ypsilantians' visions of good and meaningful work. Their accounts of how they have lived are situated in the small city, but their accounts of what they want in the future are affected by a larger city to the east and that city's unique history in the modern American economy.

As Ypsilanti is in the geographic vicinity of Detroit, the larger city's history and identity regarding work provide crucial context for the story told here. Detroit's stature as a major metropolis in twentieth-century America was not due to it ever being a traditionally glamorous city in the sense that some would consider Las Vegas, Los Angeles, or Miami Beach to be. Instead, Detroit's urban identity was grounded in its being a city that, in the most literal sense of the word, worked. For much of the twentieth century it was the model industrial American large city. In being such, its cultural as well as economic impact on southeastern Michigan was based on what the city represented in terms of work. As a result of the cultural and economic statement made by Detroit, the image of the broader southeastern Michigan region has been as a place where people came to get their hands dirty and be well paid by working in factories and other industrial settings. Hence, my consideration of low-income African Americans in Ypsilanti involves how they make sense of contemporary work and work opportunity within the context of how such activity emerged in the larger region.

This book is also an account of what does not surface in the imagination of black Americans concerning possible employment prospects and how this is shaped by their living next to the thriving small city of Ann Arbor. That city, steeped in an infrastructure of research and technology, houses the kind of work that is on the far opposite side of the divide from large-scale manufacturing. As I explore, black Ypsilantians did not often discuss Ann Arbor as a place for good jobs. Even if many seemingly successful people lived there and many of them were connected to the University of Michigan, this insight was beyond their purview. Essentially, what Ann Arbor residents do for employment and how they attain it does not gel with what is understandable and accessible to many black Ypsilantians. *From the Edge of the Ghetto*, then, is a story about struggling African Americans in a small city that is in some critical ways attached to a metropolis while simultaneously detached from its closer, more privileged neighbor. For black Ypsilantians, that neighbor strikes them as much more white, and much more white-collar, than what they find comfortable. Consequently, African Americans in Ypsilanti live in a city that both has reflected industrialism and its promise for mobility and economic security and, at least for them, appears to lag behind the postindustrial promise of contemporary America.

Telling this story about small-city African Americans in Ypsilanti achieves two ends. It provides recognition of certain dimensions of the African American experience that are not captured by concentrating on the big city. This is the case even if some of the general story of low-income African Americans in Ypsilanti involves the same patterns of hope and despair that circumscribe African America life more generally, especially in larger cities. Second, this book also sheds light on the situation for black Americans who lack access to positions of social and economic security in the postindustrial sphere. As I explore here, the dreams, hopes, and desires of low-income African Americans in Ypsilanti are tied to the city of Detroit in vast and provocative ways, while remaining distant from those that seem to fit well for residents of the more geographically proximate city of Ann Arbor. This pattern of connection and distance, which flies in the face of the explicitly geographical closeness of Ann Arbor and distance from Detroit, is illuminating. Thus, *From the Edge of the Ghetto* is about the relevance of place both geographically (what it means for African Americans to live a certain kind of the small-city experience) and temporally (what it means to stand in between the demise of industrialism and the rise of postindustrialism).

The notion that the people featured in this book live on the edge of the ghetto is a double entendre. First, even if the kind of employment that has been historically associated with Detroit lingers in their consciousness as they talk about meaningful work for themselves, they are not residents of that city, nor do most of them claim to frequent it in a highly consistent manner. Yet Detroit remains symbolically at the center of their notions of the kind of work that makes the most sense to them and of why various kinds of work associated with postindustrialism do not. Hence, they are, in a manner of speaking, on the edge of that place.

Second, their being situated next to Ann Arbor allows black Ypsilantians to see themselves as viewed by Ann Arbor residents as the most proximate source of the anxiety and discomfort often (and too often, unfairly) associated with African Americans residing in places such as Detroit. The issue of whether that anxiety and discomfort is legitimate and whether many of the kinds of readings made about Detroit by outsiders are accurate, is for another project. A point of this work, however, is that notions of the ghetto linger in both the mind-sets that black Ypsilantians believe the more privileged have about them as well as mind-sets that they have of themselves (the latter of which involve how and why the socioeconomically disadvantaged embrace such stereotypes). Thus, the application of the term *ghetto* is not meant to be an effective description of a place or a people (e.g., low-income African Americans). Rather, it is a trope for how black Ypsilantians discuss themselves and how they feel they are perceived by others. Being on the edge, then, means living in a place that is a distinct site of race, space, work, and infrastructure that contrast with the big-city perspective but also with the small, postindustrial-city perspective.

THE LOGIC OF *FROM THE EDGE OF THE GHETTO*

From the Edge of the Ghetto explores how Ypsilanti-based African Americans talk about what they understand to be the world of work in Ypsilanti and southeastern Michigan and what their hopes and dreams are in it. This book provides an account of how African Americans on the margins of secure employment think about work, work-related skills, and the means of connecting the two. The individuals considered here have had exposure to, and have experienced considerable frustration with, the world of work. While their views register that frustration, they also elucidate some keen and provocative insights into how people on the margins of work take stock of their situations and plan to confront them. In pursuing these issues this book documents what these individuals consider to be "good" jobs in American society (including why they hold those views and what they understand to be the means of accessing these jobs), what they believe is accessible work for African Americans of their class standing, their sense of their own work ethic, their assessment of their own skills and resources relevant to finding good work, and their understanding of how to employ those skills and resources to find such work.

In the course of pursuing black Ypsilantians' thoughts on these matters, *From the Edge of the Ghetto* pays explicit attention to how race and gender are configured in their thoughts. It explores why and how these individuals hold fast to the manufacturing sector as the site of future possibility even though they live on the doorstep of Ann Arbor, Michigan, a small city with a long-standing and successful investment in research and technology. Hence, as low-income black Americans in Ypsilanti are caught between past and future models of good work in America, they struggle with how to hold onto the past world of work and how to make sense of their future world.

As the next-door neighbor to Ann Arbor, Ypsilanti is also on the doorstep of privilege. Thus, its residents are not deeply buried in geographies of racial and class disadvantage, which is often the case for low-income African Americans who reside in larger cities. Instead, the disadvantaged African Americans of Ypsilanti have some visual sense of economic success and racial and class diversity, which as the following pages reveal, unfolds in provocative ways through their testimonies of what constitutes the local world of work and how they see themselves relating to it. Finally, the book offers insight into and understanding of key gender distinctions in how these individuals think about the challenges of finding work and what they imagine to be the most accessible employment prospects for them in the future.

The goal of garnering insight into how black Ypsilantians think about work and work opportunity was achieved through a pattern of serial investigations of open-ended interview data. That is, a set of common questions was asked of black Ypsilantians, and follow-up questions were tailored to the specific nature of their replies. A team of a half dozen researchers entered the field with me to conduct these interviews. In order to uncover themes and issues pertinent to black Ypsilantians, comparative analyses were conducted on their arguments and perspectives about the world of work in Ypsilanti and neighboring communities, work opportunity, strategies and resources for securing work, and visions of the good job. Men (49) were compared to women (54), as were parents

(32 men and 41 women) to nonparents (17 men and 13 women). Those age 25 and younger (39) were compared to those ages 26 to 32 (38) and those age 33 and older (26). Those who did not complete high school (17) were compared with those who only completed high school or received a general equivalency diploma (32), and each group was compared to those who received some form of postsecondary education (51), which meant anything from attending a few class sessions in community college through several semesters of enrollment without securing a degree. No college graduates were in the study.

Conceptually, *From the Edge of the Ghetto* elucidates the role of imagination in enabling as well as in limiting the capacity of people to engage the future. Imagination should be thought of here as one's possible, probable, and desirable visions of the future. It is not simply what psychologists refer to as one's sense of his or her possible self (Oyserman et al. 2004; Markus and Nurius 1986) but also a sense of possible life situations and positions. As a resource for enabling people to engage the future, imagination can be thought of as a muscle for engineering future pursuits. That muscle can be exercised or constrained by experiences encountered throughout one's life course.[3] Some black Ypsilantians appear to be malnourished or undernourished by their experience. That is, the kinds of opportunities afforded to people in the confined space of a small city have significantly factored into their limited social exposure, and this has hindered their capacity to imagine certain future opportunities, possibilities, and conditions. At a minimum, it has critically circumscribed how they do so. For black Ypsilantians, the imaginative muscle has been both developed and critically constrained by the particular kind of small-city experiences they have had.

Geography matters for how that muscle has been developed or constrained. Black Ypsilantians live in a small, economically challenged city situated near the promise represented by Ann Arbor and also the past success but current struggles of Detroit and southeastern Michigan. On the one hand, geography physically situates them in a place with less desirable work, removed from what they see as good jobs for themselves. As such, the content of their imaginations is a consequence of the kind of social isolation as well as social location that comes with living in a small city close to a site of postindustrial promise but also to one representing the demise of industrialism. Geographic location also affects their cognitive orientation, or the very manner in which black Ypsilantians realize and then talk about good jobs. For some of them, this talk does not venture far from the kinds of employment highly valued in the industrial era. Geographic location is relevant to the fact that they do not realize or talk about other kinds of opportunities (mostly associated with automation, technology, and the rise of the postindustrial era).

The imaginative muscle explored here drives what I refer to later on as the *functional self*. This vision of self, which I maintain is held by black Ypsilantians in much the same way that other, more socioeconomically privileged people hold visions of themselves, illustrates how people do not submit to an absence of agency when talking about their future. That is, no matter how deleterious they regard their situations to be, they also imagine some means of improving upon those circumstances (or else there would be no basis for living). How the functional self emerges for black Ypsilantians is revealed in how they talk about their preparedness and intentions for pursuing future possibilities. Both what they say and what they do not say becomes significant for understanding how this self unfolds.

A consequence of studying people who share much of the same fate in this small postindustrial city is that, save for gender (which is explored in detail throughout this book), there was considerable commonality on many themes and issues. The commonalities deserve attention because they define the unique and too often untold situation of small-city, low-income African Americans. Taking all of this into account, *From the Edge of the Ghetto* aims to offer an alternative to research centered on motivations and work-related values, which have too often been taken as the only relevant conceptual tools for exploring the situation of the socioeconomically disadvantaged in the world of work. The mandate of this book is to provide the residents of Ypsilanti the space to share their vision of work and work opportunity so that the breadth of the worldviews of low-income African Americans comes into the foreground. As much as doing so may draw attention to the vast severities impacting low-income African Americans, it is hoped that framing such a focus may also convey new possibilities for their transformation and uplift.

CHAPTER OVERVIEW

From the Edge of the Ghetto is divided into two parts. The first part, "Feeling the End of Industrialism," examines how place, and the work experiences that occur in it, shape visions of the good job and the constraints reflected in how that job is imagined. Chapter 1 explores my immersion in that place and then turns to presenting its physical and demographic structure. Chapter 2 explores how black Ypsilantians think about space as part of their cognitive frameworks of reality. It delves into why Ann Arbor, their close neighbor, is viewed by many with distrust and discomfort, while Detroit, which is farther away, represents familiarity.

Chapter 3 exposes how black Ypsilantians have experienced work. It reveals what working on the margins of security and opportunity has meant as a foundation for exploring how black Ypsilantians think about the future. It also explores their perceptions of the role of race in their work experiences. Race and gender are embedded and interrelated in the everyday experiences of people. They also remain mutually implicated in how people talk about those experiences. Accordingly, this chapter directly invests in an account of the gendered distinctions in how race and the work experience was discussed.

The second part of the book, "Fitting into the Postindustrial World," explores how black Ypsilantians think about future possibilities and the means to secure them. Unquestionably, the small-city experience affects how black Ypsilantians think about the future. However, the most striking feature of their thinking concerns how gendered it turns out to be. That is, despite some commonalities in their thinking, men and women make some distinct arguments about how they see themselves as employees in the future world of work. Here we see how black Ypsilantians dream as they do partly because of the limitations created by their current living and employment circumstances, but how some of them, especially the women, can see a possible better future much more clearly than can others.

Chapter 4 turns to what black Ypsilantians imagine to be good jobs for people like themselves. This focus reveals much about how they view the future because it provides some definition of their interests and desires. Chapter 5 explores how black Ypsilantians discuss their work ethic. It first draws out the discussions of work ethic as a personal philosophy and then turns to considering how black Ypsilantians explain how that ethic has surfaced in their actual work experiences. The distinction is crucial because it helps unpack and explicate a dimension of how black Ypsilantians think about themselves and their personal qualities in contrast to how they explain engaging in a life experience of marginal and often highly unfulfilling work. Chapter 6 follows that discussion by addressing the gendered distinctions in black Ypsilantians' visions of their own human resources relevant to work. Finally, the conclusion makes a statement about the interconnection of place, race, and gender for small-city African Americans.

The way in which place matters for how black Ypsilantians have contended with the end of industrialism (the focus of part I), then, serves as a foundation for their arguments about the future, which constitute efforts to fit themselves into a postindustrial world (the focus of part II). The future-focused quests of black Ypsilantians may be similar to those of struggling African Americans who live in larger cities, but their origins rest firmly in their small-city experience.

NOTES

1. It has been argued that Ann Arbor's status as such a place is due to its historic investments in research and technological development. See Levy (2010).

2. Socioeconomically challenged black Americans also have lived in suburbs and small cities throughout this period of time (Wiese 2004). Often the situations affecting black Americans in larger cities have also impacted those who lived in nearby suburbs and small towns, yet the smaller-city story, which seems less intriguing and portentous in the age of the urban underclass, has garnered less attention. However, a body of scholarship on African American poverty in small cities has recently emerged in an effort to expand the analytical view taken toward black Americans at the bottom of the socioeconomic hierarchy (Barnes 2005; Hamer 2001). Much of this work aims to document how black Americans living in these environments suffer the same plight and afflictions as do those in larger cities, yet they are not as well recognized because of the historic focus on the large city. This kind of effort is in stark contrast to that of anthropologist Carol Stack, whose *All Our Kin: Strategies for Survival in a Black Community* (1975) also centered on the small-city experiences of low-income African Americans. It is important to note, however, that the emphasis of her work was not on small-city life per se, but rather on the kinds of social exchanges and reciprocity patterns that low-income African Americans engaged in to meet the demands and challenges of their lives. These patterns could be found in large-city cases as well. Otherwise, prior to this recent turn to the African American experience in small cities, studies of the experiences of low-income individuals in small cities have often been restricted to examining the situation of white Americans (Lynd and Lynd 1929, although Murphy forthcoming offers a refreshing recent commentary on that experience).

3. I am grateful for the efforts of Aunrika Tucker-Shabazz in helping me to clarify my thinking about the imagination in this way.

Part I

Feeling the End of Industrialism

ONE

Bringing Myself to the Edge

Forty-two-year-old Jerry Jackson had worked as a custodian for most of his adult life.[1] He was born in Ann Arbor but moved to Ypsilanti as a young adult. He said that his childhood neighborhood, in public housing on the west side of Ann Arbor, was not an easy place to live. "In order to go down the street you had to fight. In order to go to school, you had to fight. So it was a pretty rough neighborhood back then."

For Jerry, life at home was not much better than life in the neighborhood. Jerry grew up in a close relationship with mother: "I guess you could say [it was like] a brother/sister relationship because I can talk to her about anything. I don't have to try and hide anything." However, his relationship with his father was much different. His father did not consistently live with him and his mother and therefore was a less frequent presence in his life. As Jerry explained, "The only thing that was negative was like when my dad was living with us. I'd watch him come home and jump on my mom for nothing, you know, for absolutely nothing." In his continual manner of speaking as if he just took life as it came to him, Jerry said, "I never asked [why he did that], you know. [I] never tried to figure it out because it seemed like it happed continuous. I never tried to figure it out."

As Jerry spoke, it was clear that he was not very long on words. In the course of his interview his facial expressions spoke as much as his voice did in presenting his vision of how his life had unfolded and how he felt about it. When telling stories about his past he would sometimes conclude his accounts with an abruptness that conveyed that what he had said was just the way things were.

Jerry began playing various sports while growing up—football, base-ball, and even hockey until it got too expensive. He played in Ann Arbor. Recalling his experiences in sports, he said, "I was called [the N-word] a lot and spit on, threw coffee on, all that kind of stuff." As a result of these experiences, Jerry said that he did not have much to do with the people of Ann Arbor. Discussing his social life as an adolescent in Ann Arbor, he said, "I just hung out with the athletes." His awareness of being less economically secure than some of his athletic peers in Ann Arbor emerged during his teenage years. He said, "They wanted new tennis shoes, they get new tennis shoes. They want a car, they got a car." Due to his mother's limited income, none of this came his way.

Immediately after completing high school Jerry landed a job at a General Motors plant and began his adult life in Ypsilanti. That job brought him his first exposure to custodial work, in a setting that provided fringe benefits. He was making what he felt was a decent salary and received benefits that enabled him to have several surgeries on his arms for what he reported was carpal tunnel syndrome. He lost that job when he was in his early twenties because, he said, his physician improperly filed paper-work about his health condition. Jerry was unable to enlist his union to help him correct the matter, and what he felt was the best job he had ever had was gone.

Since then, even though he has had several custodial jobs over time, Jerry has been struggling. He was married for seven years but got di-vorced; he has no children. He explained that his failed marriage was due to his spouse. "[She] wasn't very supportive because all she wanted to do was spend the money. When I tried to save it, you know, she had control of the checkbook. She'd just go out and write checks."

Like many African Americans in Ypsilanti, Jerry has obtained employ-ment but never consistent financial security. In the decade after he lost his job at General Motors, Jerry rarely earned more than $8.00 an hour. He said, "I've had like one that paid like $20 an hour but I didn't have the transportation to it. Therefore, I couldn't keep the job."

That job was in Southfield, a suburb immediately west of Detroit. To get to that job Jerry needed a car (at least one that did not consistently break down). This is precisely what he did not have. Despite his difficult experiences with work, he believes that good jobs exist and can be found "out there." Like many small-city residents, he also believes that transportation is vital to getting access to those jobs. In the absence of access to a major metropolitan transportation system, for him and others like him mobility requires having a car. Without one, he has had to make do with whatever can be found closer to home, and that has been custodial work. He said:

> I'm biting my tongue working for $7.50 an hour right now, you know. It's a real hard pill to swallow. Like my mom says before you walk you got to crawl, you know. I talked to her about it all the time. She says, "Son, you got a crawl before you can walk. You gotta start somewhere. Something beats nothing." That's what she tells me.

Jerry is the kind of person whom I came to better understand after spending some time with black Ypsilantians. His was the first of several stories that enabled me to grasp the powerful cultural divide between Ann Arbor and Ypsilanti. His story also helped me to understand how Ypsilanti is on the edge of both the traditional industrial sphere in Michigan and the emergent postindustrial sphere reflected by Ann Arbor.

Jerry now lives in a city that he has found to be more socially and culturally comfortable for him than the neighboring one of Ann Arbor, even though he was born and raised there. Several of the black Ypsilantians in this book also reported finding Ann Arbor to be an uncomfortable place, and most others did not reference it much at all when talking about good jobs for people like themselves. The kind of work that Jerry did in his past brought him relative material and emotional comfort because it took place in a factory, where his labor was supported by benefits safeguarded by membership in a union. Without that foundation in his more recent experiences, the kind of work he has done has allowed him to do no more than survive. Much like Jerry, many black Ypsilantians have also struggled with being located in a city not well equipped with what they believed to be good jobs.

When asked about where he believed good jobs were located, Jerry said, "Usually further out, Detroit area, you know, Inkster, stuff like that."[2] Referencing Detroit or the broader southeastern Michigan region was common among those featured in this book. Like Jerry, the other 102 participants also implied or spoke directly about the limits and constraints on securing good work as being tied to their living in Ypsilanti. Some argued that good work was to be found in or closer to Detroit, while most just argued that it could be found elsewhere in southeastern

Michigan, even if they struggled to articulate precisely where that else-where was.

The particular ways in which race, opportunity, and place matter for Jerry and the other black Ypsilantians form the crux of this story. That is because what initially might appear to be a common story of struggle for African Americans takes on a very different aspect when situated in a small city that few people have ever heard of and that is close to both a large city of past promise in America and a thriving small city that today is very promising but seemingly unfamiliar and uncomfortable to the residents of this neighboring town. The ability for black Ypsilantians to conceive of opportunity and the mechanisms for securing it is not unlike that of working-class and low-income African Americans who have expe-rienced other kinds of living (big city, suburban, or other). However, the effects of past work experiences and living conditions in the kind of small-city life that black Ypsilantians have encountered matter greatly for the content of some of their conceptions about opportunity and how well they are positioned to act upon those conceptions. I first began to under-stand this as I started personally experiencing this city on the edge.

Initially, *From the Edge of the Ghetto* was not supposed to happen. This investigation of low-income African Americans in Ypsilanti, Michigan, was intended to be a pit stop on the way to a larger study of black Americans in Detroit. I felt compelled to study Detroit because that city has been a site of extreme urban disadvantage (Adler 1995; Binelli 2012; Bergmann 2008; Boyd 2017; Leduff 2014; Sugrue 1996; Farley, Danziger, and Holzer 2000). It is not surprising to anyone interested in urban issues that Detroit is and for decades has been home to a large number of African Americans. In the last few decades of the twentieth century it became, to paraphrase urban demographer Reynolds Farley and his col-leagues (1978), one of America's prominent "chocolate" cities. This being the case, I was surprised at how few sociologists seemed to have spent time doing detailed interviews with Detroit residents about their percep-tions of economic opportunity in their city, the potential significance of race and racism for the existence and pursuit of these opportunities, and what these residents envisioned as constituting the good life.[3] Scholars had collected plenty of data about the changing racial dynamics of the city and what they had meant for its residential life, but not much else had been done in sociology about the everyday life experiences of its residents (a key exception is Farley, Danziger, and Holzer 2000). More important for me is that there had been precious little participant observational or conversational-style interviewing research, the kind upon which I have built my career (Young 1999, 2004, 2008, 2010), conducted with African American men in that city. A major factor in my choosing to accept a position on the faculty of the University of Michigan over twenty years ago was the opportunity to conduct research on black men in what I believed was one of the most understudied cities in American sociology. Hence, I came to Michigan believing it was time to tell a Detroit story about African American men and the urban experience.

As Ypsilanti is less than a 40-minute drive from downtown Detroit, my pursuit of fieldwork there emerged from my sense that the smaller city would offer an ideal laboratory for developing an approach to the queries that I intended to bring to Detroit. When first going to Ypsilanti I held steadfastly to the idea that whatever was on the minds of low-income African American men and (as I determined to investigate a bit later) women in this small city also would be on the minds of such people in Michigan's largest city. I began the Ypsilanti project believing that a few months of research there would be all that I needed to be prepared to investigate low-income African Americans in Detroit. Not only was Ypsilanti a plausible pilot test site for me because it houses an accessible constituency of low-income African Americans, but also, prior to my conducting research there it became an important place for me to meet my own interest in things African American.

When I arrived in Michigan in the summer of 1996, one of the first things I was compelled to do upon moving to this new environment was find a place to get a haircut. I brought my concern to an African American male graduate student in the University of Michigan's Department of Sociology. Without hesitation, he got on the phone and called his barber, a gentleman named Marty Moss. Marty (one of the few actual names used in this book) owned a shop in Ypsilanti called Rammos (pronounced Ray-Mows). Soon after the phone call was completed we were on our way to what was my first trip to Ypsilanti.

At the time, Rammos was located on Michigan Avenue, the main thoroughfare in Ypsilanti. The shop anchored the southwest corner of Michigan Avenue and Huron Drive, the latter being the street that traffic poured onto after exiting the interstate highway that cut across the southern end of the city. (See figure 1.1.) While I was certainly aware of Ypsi-

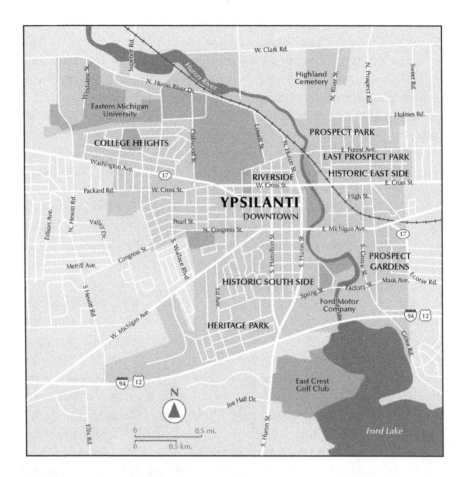

Figure 1.1. Map of Ypsilanti
Source: Referenced from Google Maps.

lanti as Ann Arbor's largest eastern neighbor, I had not yet ventured into this town to get an idea of its scenic quality or cultural flavor. However, having taken the local streets from Michigan's campus to Rammos for the first of many haircuts there, I had the opportunity to take my first serious note of the gradual change in scenery from Ann Arbor to Ypsilanti. My first image of the city was the grounds of Eastern Michigan University (EMU), a public institution of over 23,000 students, perhaps best known for producing the critical mass of the east side of the state's public school teachers. It also appeared to me to be an institution with an identity much more firmly rooted in the local community than was the University of Michigan (in large part because EMU is a commuter institution).

Although a number of small towns separate Ypsilanti from Detroit, Ypsilanti looked like the perfect kind of town to stand between that city, a hallmark of twentieth-century American industrialism, and Ann Arbor, a thriving small city reflecting many of the accoutrements of postindustrialism (a major research university being the primary example). Ypsilanti did not have the kind of developed downtown that was a core feature of the unique small-city flavor of Ann Arbor. Instead, Ypsilanti had fewer restaurants, less ostentatious houses, and—immediately recognizable to me—many more African Americans. In fact, over the years I would marvel at how often some residents of Ann Arbor and the communities that bordered its western and southern boundaries would discuss Ypsilanti as if it were the gateway to Detroit. It was obvious from their remarks that they did so because, although it was not an actual neighbor of Detroit, Ypsilanti was both less socioeconomically privileged than and housed a higher percentage of African Americans than Ann Arbor. As such, Ypsilanti bore the image of a less desirable place to live (unless one was a University of Michigan student in need of affordable housing). At the time that I first encountered Ypsilanti, however, it struck me that this city would offer me my best chance for engaging the kind of quotidian African American culture that I had not yet figured out how to find in Ann Arbor (nor was even sure existed there). This possibility became clear to me during my trip to get a haircut.

As soon as we passed through the front door of Rammos that August afternoon, I encountered the kind of cultural aura that since moving to Ann Arbor I had begun to wonder whether I would have to abandon altogether. I had moved there from Chicago, where I was a graduate student. Chicago had plenty to offer in terms of African American urban culture, and having been born and raised in New York City, which I (admittedly self-centeredly) regard as the capital of African American urban life, Rammos seemed to be as close as I was going to get to being home, at least until I knew much more about the town to which my spouse and I had moved.

The layout of the barbershop was a column of barber chairs on the left-hand side of the shop as one entered the place and a column of chairs for waiting customers facing the barber chairs. A few other barber chairs were located upstairs, accessed by a staircase located immediately behind the column of waiting chairs. Marty served his own customers in the first barber chair on the ground floor, right behind a plate glass window that, together with the glass door, comprised the establishment's storefront.

The barbershop was not extraordinarily crowded on the day of my first visit. Only a few customers were on hand. Every barber and all of the customers were African American, and the conversations and verbal banter disseminating throughout the place ranged from sports to politics to neighborhood affairs. The four or so barbers at work that day were pivots for the conversations. They directed remarks made by particular customers to others sitting in waiting chairs or to other barbers. Often they simply added their own embellishment or critique to whatever topic was on the floor. It was not so much the topics for discussion but the manner in which the men at Rammos affirmed their claims, disputed or accepted those of others, and made facial expressions and gesticulations that allowed me to feel as though I had encountered a social milieu that was traditionally African American, yet also was only a few miles away from my first home outside of big-city America. I left Rammos that afternoon feeling gratified at having received a haircut, having met Marty (who nearly twenty years later continues to cut whatever remaining hair I have, as well as that of my two sons), and having encountered what I regarded as my first "black" social space since moving to Michigan.

In the years following my first visit to that barbershop, Ypsilanti also became important to me because it was home to a small take-out restaurant located about a half mile south of the barbershop (near Huron River Drive, but closer to the interstate highway). Until my dietary practices changed in later years, I visited this restaurant on a near biweekly basis to pick up fried chicken and a selection of soul food side dishes. The restaurant was located on a small lot in a trailer-sized structure, positioned just behind a gas station (and situated such that anyone unfamiliar with the area could easily drive right past the restaurant without knowing that it existed). Upon entering through the front door of this shop, customers faced a bulletproof glass enclosure that necessitated speaking loudly so that their orders could be heard (although regular customers knew to call in their orders ahead of time, as the chicken was cooked to order, requiring a 20-minute wait). The glass enclosure was reminiscent of those found in the Chinese take-out restaurants that I had frequented in Harlem and the Bronx many years before. Finding a place in Ypsilanti that produced fried chicken similar to what I had consumed in New York made this city register even more fully in my mind as a crucial place for my cultural sustenance.

At the same time that I found Ypsilanti to be a place for making cultural connections, I also became intrigued about what struck me as unique and different about that city in comparison to other "African American" places that I had lived in or frequented. That is, the smallness of Ypsilanti is such that I would never mistake it for New York City or Chicago. In many ways, Ypsilanti felt to me like a large neighborhood rather than a city. In part, this was because it seemed as if other than visiting Detroit, a fair number of the African Americans whom I encountered there had never experienced large-city life. Furthermore, while parts of Ypsilanti were quite residentially segregated, I never acquired a sense that Ypsi (as it is commonly called by southeastern Michiganders) housed an institutional ghetto or a neighborhood or community setting that was home to a variety of African American social and cultural institutions in the way that Harlem, Brooklyn, and the south side of Chicago are.[4] Instead, Ypsilanti seemed to have places like Rammos on one block, the take-out soul food restaurant located about a half mile away, and a few stores located elsewhere that catered to African American interests. In between these businesses were institutions that served the public, such as the city hall, which was located almost exactly on the straight line connecting Rammos to the fried chicken shop. This pattern disrupted a sense of geographic continuity in the residential and social spaces occupied by African Americans in larger cities. As the businesses owned by and/or catering to African Americans were distributed across the geographical landscape, I never embraced the notion that black Americans in Ypsilanti experienced the kind of sociogeographic isolation that unfolded in many larger American cities and that actually gave rise to the emergence and perseverance of institutional ghettoes in the first place.

Despite this geographic particularity, I remained quite aware of—and took comfort in—the fact that the black Americans I encountered in Ypsilanti listened to the music that African Americans in large cities listened to, told jokes in much the same way that those others did (although lacking the cadence of New York City–style street corner banter), and talked about the same political and social issues that held the interest of the people I had encountered in East Harlem and Chicago. In some striking ways, then, the African American cultural flow of Ypsilanti was both different from and the same as that of New York City or Chicago. That duality was lodged in my thinking when I began planning to conduct my pilot research in that city.

After developing a framework for a research agenda, I soon discovered that one strong similarity between Ypsilanti and larger American cities is that they have all served as sites for twentieth-century African Americans to realize the American Dream. Ypsilanti had been home to some of the automobile manufacturing plants that provided secure and materially rewarding blue-collar employment throughout much of the twentieth century. In the early to mid-twentieth century it was also a place of significance for African American and white American families from Alabama and the Appalachian regions of eastern Kentucky because many such people left those areas to secure employment in Ypsilanti's automobile manufacturing sector. Accordingly, Ypsilanti was a place of promise and possibility for African Americans throughout the early and mid-twentieth century. Eventually I came to understand that promise and possibility in Ypsilanti took shape nearly a hundred years before the start of that century.

A BRIEF HISTORY OF YPSILANTI

The territory that eventually became Ypsilanti was formally settled in 1823. Before that the territory was used as a trading post by French explorers and other settlers in the region. It soon came to be regarded as a potential conduit between the cities of Chicago and Detroit. In 1823 Benjamin Woodruff and some companions who used the post established a settlement called Woodruff's Grove. This settlement, which allowed for the formal appointment of a postmaster to direct the distribution of mail, paved the way for the emerging city (Marshall 1993). In the first few years after 1823 other settlers arrived to acquire land and establish small businesses. They included people of French, Indian, and what is regarded today as African American ancestry.

In 1825 Judge August Brevoort Woodward, a settler who had acquired 600 acres of territory that one day would become part of Michigan Avenue, attended a community meeting with fellow settlers in the region in order to establish a name for what had expanded far beyond a mere trading post. Woodward convincingly argued for a name that came from General Demetrius Ypsilanti, a Greek military leader who had led 300 troops out of harm's way at night after being confronted by 30,000 Turkish soldiers in the Greek War of Independence in the 1820s.

In 1824 Father Gabriel Richard, a Catholic priest and representative to the US Congress from what was then formally known as the Michigan Territory, urged the building of a federal route to replace the Sauk Indian Trail. That trail had been selected by the US government as the first road between Chicago and Detroit. The federal route, established by 1839, was initially named Chicago Road. It later became Michigan Avenue, and it runs across the entire state of Michigan. Upon reaching Ypsilanti, about 180 miles from its western point of origin in Michigan, the avenue runs straight through the downtown portion of the city. It is the site of much of Ypsilanti's commercial activity, including the buildings housing city hall, the police department, a number of fast-food and family-style restaurants, and a car dealership. A second commercial district, Depot Town, exists about half a mile north of the Michigan Avenue strip and was first created in the early part of the nineteenth century (the prominence of this space was enhanced by the establishment of a railroad station there in 1838). That area houses a few bars and local eateries, and throughout the first decade of the twenty-first century it was the site of a revival centered on the formal sanctioning of Depot Town as a historic district.

From the 1800s until the early part of the twentieth century, Ypsilanti's location on the Huron River allowed its economy to develop as paper and lumber mills proliferated, and factories producing various goods, including cigars and underwear, were built. This production was overshadowed by Henry Ford, who brought automotive manufacturing to Ypsilanti in the late 1930s and established Ford Motor Company's Willow Run plant in 1941.[5] From that period into the 1980s, Ypsilanti's economic fortune was tied to the automobile industry.

The history of the black American presence in Ypsilanti is about as long as that of the city itself. According to Ypsilanti historian Albert P. Marshall (1993), the US census of 1830 reported a small number of "people of color" living there. The census report of 1840 indicates that 58 African Americans were residents of the city. Many were migrants from the northeast who strove to escape the congestion (at least as it was regarded by the residents in that period of time) that was emerging in that region's urban core. An African American institutional sphere slow-

ly emerged, beginning with the formation of the African Methodist Episcopal Society of Ypsilanti in 1848.

The small number of African Americans in Ypsilanti meant that racial
conflict was minimal for much of the first few years of the history of that
city. When Michigan became a formal state in 1837, however, voting
rights were denied to those of African American descent. As black
Americans continued to arrive in Ypsilanti, many of them skilled crafts-
men from the East Coast, and as Ypsilanti became a pivotal point along
the route to Canada for the Underground Railroad, a heightened political
efficacy was cultivated among African Americans in that city as well as a
mild tolerance, if not overt acceptance, of them by the white Americans
who settled there.

Ypsilanti's black Americans supported the Union during the Civil
War, and many African Americans began to migrate to the city following
the end of the war and the abolition of slavery. Many such migrants
found work in the agricultural arena, while others began entrepreneurial
ventures in that sector. By the late 1880s Ypsilanti was home to nearly 500
African Americans and was regarded as a more desirable place to live
than was neighboring Ann Arbor, which by that time had begun to acquire an identity as an elite residential community that was less accepting
of African American residents. Ypsilanti's status as a desirable place to
live facilitated its growth throughout the twentieth century. Between
1930 and 1970 the population of the city increased by 91.2%, from 10,143
to 29,538.[6] A primary cause for this growth was Ypsilanti's success as a
single-industry town. As in much of southeastern Michigan, automobile
manufacturing was the source of gainful employment. During World
War II efforts to build cars were interrupted by the conversion of an
automobile plant into the Willow Run Bomber Plant. This plant produced
the B-24 bombers that were a tremendous resource for the American
efforts in the war. The employment opportunities that came with the
plant, which was reconverted back to automobile manufacturing after the
war, resulted in a severe housing shortage.

Throughout the early and middle part of the twentieth century Ypsi-
lanti, like much of Michigan, benefited from the manufacturing plants
established by the major American automobile manufacturers: the Ford
Motor Company, the Chrysler Corporation (which became the Daimler-
Chrysler Corporation in 1998), and the General Motors Corporation.
Ypsilanti residents benefited from the proliferation of manufacturing

plants in or near the city, and many black Americans surely took advantage of those prospects. In fact, Ford's Willow Run Bomber Plant, located immediately north of Ypsilanti, employed more than 100,000 people.

During the middle of the twentieth century migrants from the South and the Appalachian region came to Ypsilanti and its surrounding communities seeking secure blue-collar work in the automobile industry. As a result of the employment boom, many families migrated to Ypsilanti and the broader region, thus causing for some time a severe housing shortage. However, the next twenty years were a period of regional decline for the automobile industry, during which the city experienced a population decrease, falling from 29,538 to 24,818 (a 16% population loss) from 1970 to 1990.[7]

Two high points in the history of Ypsilanti occurred in the 1960s, neither having to do with what was an eventual downward pattern in the quality of life for many of the city's African Americans. One began in 1960 when brothers Tom and James Monaghan bought a pizza restaurant, originally named DomiNicks, located just east of the campus of EMU. Soon after making the transaction, James sold his half of the restaurant to his brother (presumably because he did not want to sacrifice his job as a postal worker for a risky entrepreneurial activity), and by 1965 Tom had acquired two other pizza restaurants in Washtenaw County (the location of Ypsilanti and Ann Arbor). The original owner forbade Tom to continue using the name DomiNicks, so the new name became one that an employee suggested, Domino's. What began with a $500 down payment and a $900 loan to buy a store in Ypsilanti became an international pizza enterprise now known throughout the country and parts of the world (Sloane and Monaghan 2003).

The second high point began with a realization made by David Weikart, a mid-twentieth-century school administrator in the Ypsilanti public school system. While at work Weikart noticed the chronic underperformance of low-income African American youth in that system. He saw that these children were consistently assigned to special education classes, were held back from advancing to later grades, and failed to complete high school. He decided to embark upon establishing a preschool that would involve experimental education efforts for young children, including having parents read to their children at home and having them read back to their parents. He also encouraged children to be charged with counting the change received by their parents when they shopped in local stores. Most important, he mandated that children begin formal schooling at the age of three or four. His objective was to take note of the development of the children years after their participation in the specialized preschool that he created to enforce each of these activities.

The school that housed this program was formally named the Perry Preschool (named in 1956 after Dr. Lawrence C. Perry, a local dentist, community leader, and Ypsilanti school board member who died in 1955). The Perry Preschool opened in October 1962 and operated for five years, with a new group of children entering each fall. The efforts unfolding in the Perry Preschool informed an initiative launched by President Lyndon Baines Johnson in 1965: the federal preschool program known as Head Start (Schweinhart 2004; Schweinhart and Weikart 1997). The foundings of Domino's Pizza and Head Start remain part of the hidden history of Ypsilanti. Even if these facts are well known to historians of culinary arts and education, they are hidden in that few residents whom I talked to knew about either of them, and neither seems to reflect much about contemporary life in Ypsilanti.

CONTEMPORARY YPSILANTI

Ypsilanti nowadays appears to be a prototypical post-automobile-industry town. Its history is marked by the rise and decline of that industry. Throughout the twentieth century its spacious fields and farms were transformed into automobile and manufacturing plants and businesses that served the workers in those settings (Peterson 2002). By 2000, aside from a smattering of discount stores, service shops, and small churches, Ypsilanti appeared to be a locale for abandoned stores and empty space. Since then it has become virtually two kinds of residential communities in one small city. The community of concern in *From the Edge of the Ghetto* is largely African American and poor. The other, largely white American and considerably more economically secure, is a bedroom community for Ann Arbor, its western neighbor. For many of its residents, and especially for its African American inhabitants, by the year 2000, rather than appearing to be an economically vibrant small city, Ypsilanti had become a small city that needed help to become vibrant once again. The contemporary situation of black Ypsilantians is circumscribed by the last two decades of change in Ypsilanti in terms of population, employment, and general quality of life indicators.[8]

Employment Trends and Patterns

By 1990 Ypsilanti was a small city struggling to fit into the postindustrial era. The engine of the decline in the quality of life was the demise of automobile-related manufacturing. From 1990 to 2000 Ypsilanti lost over 2,000 jobs (US Census Bureau and Social Explorer 2000). In 1990, 13,565 of the 21,214 residents over the age of 16 were employed (US Census Bureau 1990), two-thirds of them in blue-collar jobs, about half of which were in service occupations. Another 20% were in administrative/clerical work, and the final 13% were machine operators. The industries in which these jobs were located included durable manufacturing, health services, retail trade, and educational services (US Census Bureau and Social Explorer 1990). In 2000 the employment distribution remained about the same. In that year 12,784 of the 19,193 residents over the age of 16 were employed, two-thirds of them in blue-collar jobs, about 40% of those in service occupations, 11% in administrative and clerical work, and 5% in transportation (US Census Bureau 2000c).

By 2005 the most common industries in Ypsilanti were educational services, retail trade, and manufacturing. In that year, 63% of the jobs were in manufacturing, education services, and health care and social assistance.[9] According to the American Community Survey, as of 2010 the major industries included health care and social assistance (36.3%), retail trade (16.1%), arts and entertainment (14.8%), and manufacturing (7.4%). Collectively these four industries accounted for almost 75% of the businesses operating in Ypsilanti in that year.[10] It is estimated that between the years 2005 and 2035, health-care and education services will increase by 3,120 and 1,008 jobs, respectively. However, manufacturing — once the bread and butter of economic life in Ypsilanti and the sector of work most familiar to black Ypsilantians — will decrease by 845 jobs (making up less than 2% of jobs in 2035, compared to slightly less than 10% in 2005) (SEMCOG 2010).

In 2015 the labor force participation rate for those age 16 and above — a measurement of those either at work or actively seeking work — was 68.3% (57.5% being employed and 10.8% unemployed). About 31% of that population was not in the labor force (US Census Bureau and Social Explorer 2013). While no one particular sector has replaced the manufacturing jobs lost in the city, several sectors have begun to emerge, including small manufacturing and craft production, the creative/leisure economy, and renewable energy and food.[11]

The declining quality of the employment situation in modern-day Ypsilanti is also reflected by measures of income and poverty. In 1990 Ypsilanti median per capita individual annual income was $10,655, which is lower than the immediately surrounding areas of Ypsilanti Township as well as Washtenaw County. At that time, 18.2% of Ypsilanti families lived below the poverty line, and average per household annual income stood at $21,219. That was significantly lower than was the case for Washtenaw County, where the household income level in 1990 was $36,307.[12] By 1999, 42.4% of African American residents lived at or below the poverty line (US Census Bureau and Social Explorer 1990, 2000).

At the dawn of the twenty-first century Ypsilanti experienced a small decrease in its poverty rates for individuals (–2.8%) and households (–2.9%). Yet those living in poverty still made up a significant portion of the population. As of 2000 about 20% of individuals and almost 25% of households live in poverty. More data reveal sustained rates of poverty. As of 2010, 34.2% of households were headed by women. Moreover, 10.7% of residents were unemployed and over 30% were not in the labor force (SEMCOG 2010).

In 2000 the estimated median household income was $28,610. According to 2000 census measures, 4,767 people (and 2,054 households), or nearly 26% of the population (and 24% of the households) whose income status could be determined by the US Census Bureau were living below the poverty level (US Census Bureau 2000; SEMCOG 2006). Per household annual income stood at $16,692 in 2000. In 2009 the per capita income for individuals was $18,838, and per household income stood at $24,777 (US Census Bureau 2000a; SEMCOG 2010). Not much had changed by 2013. At that time the median household income was $31,454, and 31.5% of Ypsilanti families lived below the poverty level. For those whose poverty status could be determined, 53.7% of children under the age of 18 and 34.2% of those ages 18 to 64 lived below the poverty level (US Census Bureau and Social Explorer 2013).

Demographic Trends and Patterns

In equal measure to what transpired in employment, Ypsilanti went through some critical demographic shifts between 1990 and 2000. It experienced an 8% decrease in the white population and a 5.5% increase in the black population during that period. In 2000 Ypsilanti consisted of about 22,362 people spread over 4.51 square miles. About 6,838 of its residents, or 30.6%, were African American (Caucasians making up 61.4%, or 13,731 residents) (US Census Bureau 2000a). Through 2010 the proportion of African American residents remained at around 30%, although the actual number of African Americans declined to just under 5,669 (US Census Bureau 2000a). As of 2013, Ypsilanti was home to 19,693 residents, of whom 59% were white American and 31.8% African American (US Census Bureau and Social Explorer 2013).

It is not unusual for upturns in poverty and socioeconomic blight to be matched by upturns in crime and delinquency. For Ypsilanti at the turn of the century, the frequency of violent crime may have appeared to be low, given the smallness of the city, but it was high in proportion to its size. From 1999 through 2004, the police documented 10 murders, 116 rapes, and 344 robberies. More tellingly, the annual crime index, which is a measure of the number of crimes in eight categories (willful homicide, forcible rape, robbery, burglary, aggravated assault, larceny over $50, motor vehicle theft, and arson) committed per 100,000 residents in a geographic region, varied between 397.6 and 484.5 during these years. The average for the United States as a whole during that period was in the low 300s.[13]

Finally, the story of contemporary Ypsilanti includes its measures of educational attainment. In 1990 about 44% of Ypsilanti residents age 25 and older did not graduate from high school. Among the 56.4% of the residents who did graduate, 43.4% only graduated from high school, 43.8% received some college education or an associate's degree, and 12.8% graduated from college. The measure of those who did not graduate from high school had dropped to 29.5% by 2000. Among Ypsilanti's entire population in 2000, 64.7% had less than a college degree. Of those, 33% had a high school diploma or less (US Census Bureau and Social Explorer 1990, 2000).

In 2010, of the population age 25 or older (estimated at 9,881), 89.1% had completed high school or received a general equivalency diploma (GED). About 71% of the estimated population had attended some college, and 35.9% possessed a college degree (17.3% possessed an advanced degree: MA, PhD, or professional school degree) (US Census Bureau and Social Explorer 2013).

The Deep Pocket of Poverty in Ypsilanti

The southwestern part of Ypsilanti is composed of Census Tracts 4106, 4107, and 4108 (see figure 1.2) (US Census Bureau and Social Explorer 1990). These are the most socioeconomically deprived sections of the city. They are also where many African Americans in Ypsilanti reside, including almost all of the people featured in this book (some live very close by).

In tract 4106, the heart of the residential space occupied by many people featured in this book, 89.6% of the 2,992 residents living there in 1990 were African American. That number had dropped to 2,624 by 2000, with African Americans remaining at nearly 90% of the population. Of those age 25 and older, 44% had not graduated from high school in 1990,

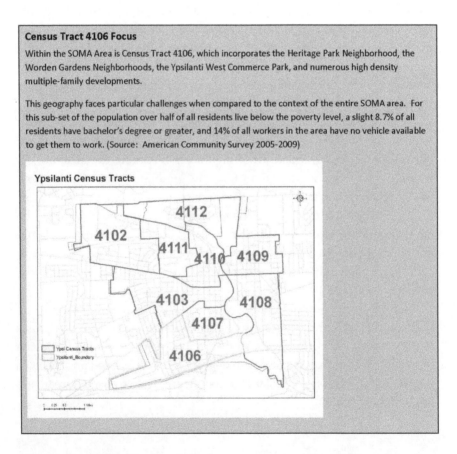

Census Tract 4106 Focus

Within the SOMA Area is Census Tract 4106, which incorporates the Heritage Park Neighborhood, the Worden Gardens Neighborhoods, the Ypsilanti West Commerce Park, and numerous high density multiple-family developments.

This geography faces particular challenges when compared to the context of the entire SOMA area. For this sub-set of the population over half of all residents live below the poverty level, a slight 8.7% of all residents have bachelor's degree or greater, and 14% of all workers in the area have no vehicle available to get them to work. (Source: American Community Survey 2005-2009)

Figure 1.2. Ypsilanti Census Tracts
Source: City of Ypsilanti Planning and Development Department 2011.

and 29.5% had not in 2000. About 41.7% of those who were age 15 or older in 1990 had been married at some point in their lives, as had about 50.6% of those who were age 15 or older in 2000 (US Census Bureau and Social Explorer 1990, 2000). In 2000, among the 70% who had graduated, 27.9% had experienced some college and 2.4% had received a BA or higher degree.

By 2010 about 37.7% of those age 15 or older in Census Tract 4106 had been married at some point in their lives (US Census Bureau 2006–2010). Those age 25 and older who had not graduated from high school constituted 28.9% of the tract's population. Among those who had graduated from high school or received a GED (71.1%), 30.2% had only graduated from high school, 27.7% had received some college education, and 6.3% had received a BA or higher degree (US Census Bureau 2006–2010).

In 1990, 39.4% of families in Census Tract 4106 were living in poverty. About 94% of those families were African American. In addition, nearly two-thirds of the families living in poverty (62.1%) were headed by females. By 2010 there were 1,763 African American residents in the tract, making up 76.3% of its population (US Census Bureau 2010). In 1990, 31% of the residents over the age of 16 were employed, two-thirds of them in blue-collar jobs, working in service occupations (about a third), administrative/clerical work (about 20%), and as machine operators (13%) (US Census Bureau 1990). The industries of employment included durable manufacturing, health services, retail trade, and educational services. In 2000, 44.5% of residents over the age of 16 were employed, two-thirds of them in blue-collar jobs, about 40% of those in service occupations, 11% in administrative and clerical work, and 5% in transportation. The industries of employment remained the same. In 1999, 39.4% of families lived below the poverty level, almost all families headed by a single female (US Census Bureau and Social Explorer 1990, 2000).

We now turn to the public housing situation in Ypsilanti. The city has a small stock of public housing that serves low-income residents. Buildings with fewer than five floors are scattered throughout southwestern Ypsilanti, and together with Section 8 housing and scattered-site facilities, these constitute the public housing for the city. The Ypsilanti Housing Commission (YHC) owns and manages 198 public housing units within the city. The YHC is a federally subsidized government agency that administers public housing and Section 8 programs throughout the city of Ypsilanti. It is also the general partner of the Hamilton Crossing development, located just north of Interstate 94. Located on South Hamilton Street near the interstate highway, the Parkview Housing Complex was developed in 1970 through a partnership between the federal government's Department of Housing and Urban Development (HUD) and the Ann Arbor-Ypsilanti Negro Business and Professional League. Its purpose was to provide housing for low-income individuals. The complex had 144 units. Parkridge Homes, located at the intersection of First Court and Armstrong, was built in 1943 and consists of 77 units spread across 21 buildings (including the management office). Paradise Manor, located on the western edge of Michigan Avenue, was built in 1970 and has 35 units spread across 13 buildings. Hollow Creek, located about a mile east of Parkridge, has 23 units, and the Towner Houses consist of 26 units. Approximately 50 units of scattered-site housing exist throughout the city as well. These were established in the 1960s in about 17 different buildings.

The four major public housing developments in Ypsilanti are located in or immediately adjacent to Census Tract 4106. The region of the city where many of the individuals featured in this book reside contains a series of gated public housing developments made up of three-story buildings, each divided into apartments. The housing developments are separated by streets that contain small one- and two-story private houses, many in need of structural repair. A proliferation of weeds can be found growing out of the cracks in the sidewalks. In this part of the city, abandoned vehicles and debris litter many of the streets.

The major housing developments managed by the YHC include Parkridge Homes (with one- to three-bedroom units), Hollow Creek (two- to four-bedroom units), and Paradise Manor (two- to four-bedroom units). A slew of scattered-site housing units also exists in Ypsilanti.

The Parkview Housing Complex, acquired by the YHC in 2012, is located within walking distance of the other public housing sites and to those unfamiliar with the management of housing for low-income residents would have appeared to be a traditional Ypsilanti public housing development prior to its formal incorporation into the YHC.

The southwestern parts of the city contain swaths of private houses that at one time housed the employees of the Ypsilanti automobile plant facing Interstate 94 and other related businesses. The decline in employment prospects meant a subsequent decline in the ability to maintain these houses. Many appear worn and damaged, some so much that the public housing stock nearby appears to be a better residential option.

Near the northern edge of this part of town is Michigan Avenue. Traveling east for about a half mile on the part of the avenue that borders the low-income census tracts leads to a road that if taken for a quarter mile south brings one to the interstate highway. Traveling east for about 30 miles on the interstate highway takes one past a number of small cities and towns and then into the southern part of Detroit (as would traveling east on Michigan Avenue for that same distance, albeit having to deal with traffic lights, pedestrians, and the slower speed limits while traveling through residential communities). Hence, Ypsilanti is within a 40-minute drive of much of Detroit. Its residents can readily access employment opportunities in large portions of the Detroit metropolitan area (provided they have adequate transportation) as well as in Ann Arbor and the other small cities and townships that comprise Washtenaw and Wayne Counties.

FROM YPSILANTI TO ANN ARBOR

West of Ypsilanti is the city of Ann Arbor. In 2000 it was home to 114,024 residents. At that time its population was 74% white and 9% African American. While Ypsilanti has been a proverbial automobile city, Ann Arbor has been known as a knowledge-based, high-technology city. The former reflects the decline of industrial production in the United States, while the latter demonstrates the rise of a technological service–based economy. In 2000 the median annual income of a household in Ann Arbor was $46,299, and approximately 16% of the population lived below the official poverty line. By contrast, in Ypsilanti at the same time the median income of a household was $28,610, and more than 25% of the population lived below the poverty line (US Census Bureau 2000b, 2003).

The spacious parks and numerous research and technological firms located throughout Ann Arbor offer a contrast to much of Ypsilanti, which maintains a considerably smaller and less-developed downtown region, housing of lesser quality than that available in Ann Arbor (except for select neighborhoods, many of which are located on the western edge of Ypsilanti), and a sequence of Census Tracts just south of the downtown area that are populated by low-income African Americans who live in public housing or homes that appear more or less dilapidated. As

Ypsilanti and Ann Arbor share a public transportation system, access to the latter is much easier than to Detroit.

In the latter half of the twentieth century Ann Arbor experienced significant growth in technology, research and development, and information-based jobs (Dolgon 1994). As the site of a knowledge-based economy, Ann Arbor benefits from the University of Michigan's brokerage of partnerships and relationships between researchers and industry. Consequently, Ann Arbor has a disproportionate number of residents with university degrees. Alongside these advantages, Ann Arbor has become a locale for restaurants and shopping centers that draw customers from southeastern Michigan. People with less economic means have been priced out of Ann Arbor. Consequently, Ypsilanti and some of the surrounding communities have become residential sites for those individuals. As anthropologist Kimberly A. Clum (2008) put it in her study of the intersection of family and work in the lives of Ypsilanti-based, low-income single mothers, as Ann Arbor's economic development has accelerated its whiteness in relation to Ypsilanti, the latter has experienced accelerated blackness in the region.[14]

The acceleration of blackness in Ypsilanti is what drew me to that city so soon after my arrival in Ann Arbor. In the years that I have resided there I have come to understand how racial, ethnic, and cultural diversity surface in Ann Arbor. However, Ypsilanti continues to strike me as a place that more easily settles with low-income African Americans and the kind of cultural dynamics associated with them. This being the case, I pursued this project with a firm belief that positive development for black Ypsilantians must involve their being connected to the kind of work world most reflected by Ann Arbor. Admittedly this is implicated in the analytical lens I bring to the arguments that follow. However, it does not mean that Ann Arbor can or should save Ypsilanti, especially its African American residents. It does mean that my vision of possibility is greatly informed by how I live in and experience Ann Arbor, especially as a member of its knowledge community.

FROM PILOT PROJECT TO BOOK

This work took the form of a complete project in Ypsilanti after I received support from the University of Michigan's Poverty Research and Training Center. This center ultimately evolved into the National Poverty Center in Michigan's Gerald R. Ford School of Public Policy. Just before that evolution unfolded, I began working with a colleague who was then a postdoctoral fellow at the Poverty Research and Training Center and was beginning to craft a study of low-income African Americans. We launched the project in late 1999, and a full-scale study of low-income African Americans in Ypsilanti was under way. We worked with a team of graduate students to conduct interviews until 2002, and I continued to engage some of the people featured in this book until 2008.[15]

As with any research initiative, there were several false starts in collecting data. I initially reached out to organizations and canvassed neighborhoods in order to secure research participants. Few emerged in this way. The pace of involvement changed for the better when I met the coordinator for community outreach for the YHC. After an introductory phone call, he invited me to meet him in the community room of the Paradise Manor housing development. I had driven by the complex, located behind steel gates on Michigan Avenue, numerous times before actually setting foot in it, so at least I knew where I was going. It had been clear to me since my first glimpse of Paradise Manor from my car that its residents were living far from great lives. This was immediately obvious when I entered the complex and saw it up close.

After I parked my car on the grounds, I was approached by an elderly gentleman. I figured that he had determined from my facial expression that I was not exactly sure what I was looking for. He had a hard and wrinkled face, and the scent of liquor was on his breath, but neither prevented him from responding quite warmly when I asked him about the location of the community room. He said, "You here to see Mr. Wesley [a pseudonym]?" As soon as I told him that, indeed, I was here to see Mr. Wesley, I got the sense that he and others standing outside that day had been awaiting my arrival. The gentleman took me to a first-floor room in one of the buildings near the back of the complex. He invited me to sit down and relax and said that Mr. Wesley would be there soon.

I entered a room filled with toys, small television sets, and various gadgets (many appearing to be broken). As I took stock of the room, some of the bystanders walked past the entrance, stared at me for a short while, and said hello only after I greeted them. My presence was an unusual moment in the everyday for these people, and they seemed intrigued without trying to satisfy their curiosity in too assertive a manner. The patience they demonstrated was a bit different than what I had encountered while working in Chicago and would encounter (at a much later time) in Detroit, where more people in the larger cities were prone to ask what I was up to or else to engage in conversation with me as soon as I showed up to conduct research. In Ypsilanti I was stared and smiled at, as if it would be against some unwritten rule for the residents to engage me more directly. I decided at that point that small-city poverty must affect people's agency in this way, making them more passive, whereas people in bigger cities seemed to be a bit more assertive.

Mr. Wesley showed up about a half hour after my arrival. An athletic, brown-skinned, and mustached man who looked every bit the part of the former collegiate basketball player that he was, he shook my hand and thanked me for coming by. He also expressed his interest in helping me connect with the people that I wanted to for this study. I recall him greeting almost everyone who was in the courtyard between the buildings by name, and this, as much as anything else that I experienced, affirmed my sense of what smallness meant for a low-income community. He also said that he was not sure how much I would get from talking to some of the low-income people in Ypsilanti because, as he saw it, many of them "really just keep to themselves."

Of course he could not know that if this were all they did, it would still be of interest to me. I took note that there might be something different about small-city African Americans that was worth paying attention to. As a former resident of two of the largest cities in the country, each with robust and renowned African American communities, I never believed it possible that anyone functioning in an African American community could fully keep to themselves. Life in larger-city poverty necessitated some consistent kinds of social engagement, even if only to minimize encounters with dangerous or threatening situations by making oneself familiar with the neighbors or knowledgeable about exactly what to avoid in the neighborhood.

After 15 minutes of conversation, I followed Mr. Wesley as we drove to three of the other public housing developments and walked through them. In addition to Paradise Manor, this tour included the Parkridge Homes, Hollow Creek, and Towner. We also briefly visited some social service agencies within a short walk of some of these developments. After the tour and conversation, it was clear that access to a population for the study that I wanted to conduct would no longer be a significant problem. Mr. Wesley had established access at an employment training center that became one of two primary sites for data collection for this project. What I had anticipated would be a small-scale research project involving a few dozen interviews became a collaborative data-collection endeavor resulting in 103 cases.

Many of the unemployed and underemployed residents who provided the interviews for this book were found at the local branch of a statewide training and employment services center initiative called Michigan Works![16] The Ypsilanti branch is located across the street from the Hamilton Crossing development, near the northeast corner of Harriet and Hamilton Streets. The site is housed in a satellite branch of Washtenaw County Community College. Michigan Works! was the first statewide, unified workforce development system in the United States. Created in 1987, it served as a model to other states and has been emulated as a result of its widespread and long-standing success in its region. The system is made up of 25 regional Michigan Works! programs that, according to its own promotional materials, focus on the needs of job makers and develop talent for the twenty-first-century economy. Each Michigan Works! agency is designed to be locally responsive and demand driven, is governed by a Workforce Development Board composed of private sector representatives and local elected officials, provides services to help businesses find the skilled workers they need, and provides a competitive advantage for job seekers. At the Ypsilanti center services include resume development, job interview preparation, one-stop job placement assistance, and related services. On any weekday, the waiting room of the Harriet Street Center was filled with the kind of people who are featured in this book.

103 BLACK YPSILANTIANS

Individual portraits of the participants are provided in the appendix. Following is a general overview of them. The respondents ranged in age from 18 to 43. This reflects the wide gap in exposure to the last phase of industrial Ypsilanti. The oldest black Ypsilantians reported seeing their parents and grandparents go to work in factories and plants, almost always in the automobile industry. The youngest reported hearing about their older relatives having such work experiences, but almost never reported actually witnessing those relatives going to such jobs. The oldest,

then, have witnessed some change, while the youngest have only encountered a postindustrial Ypsilanti.

Almost 50% of the black Ypsilantians presented here had at least some
postsecondary coursework, and 46% had a high school diploma or less
(the schooling of 3% is unaccounted for). Only 17 failed to complete high
school or to receive a GED (see table 1.1). Just under 50% of the respondents were employed at the time of the interview. About 50% had held
two or more jobs over the course of their lives, and about 7% had never
been employed. (See table 1.2.) Of those who had worked, they most
often did so in food services (including fast food, grocery stores, and
short-order cookery, where 14% of the participants had held employment
at some point in their lives), office support (including clerical, administrative assistance, and reception service, where 14% had held employment), health services (including nurse's aide and patient care, where
13% had held employment), nonfood-related retail employment (including customer service, store clerk, and cashier, where 12% had held employment), and custodial services (where 11% had held employment).
(See tables 1.3 and 1.4.) The retail sector, including food- and nonfood-
related services and health services involving retail trade, accounted for
52% of the kinds of jobs black Ypsilantians held. Half of them also had
pursued education beyond receipt of a high school diploma. Nine of the
participants reported having been incarcerated (see table 1.5).

This overview makes clear that the black Ypsilantians considered here
are what anthropologist Katherine Newman (2000) describes as the
working poor. This is a mainstay, if understudied, segment of the African
American community. Newman states that a working poor family of
four earns between $20,000 and $40,000 per year (equivalent to
$30,000–$60,000 per year in 2018).[17] This salary allows them to meet basic
needs, but they also often have to go into debt in order to manage the
demands of their households. Much like the chronically poor in urban
America, the working poor function without the support of family and
friends who are firmly embedded in the world of work, and they live in
neighborhoods that are sites of decline if not decay. However, they are
neither the most downtrodden nor the least credentialed of African
American urban dwellers because they work, even if only inconsistently.

Table 1.1. Education

Education level	All	Men	Women
Some HS	17 (16.5%)	8 (16%)	9 (17%)
GED/HS grad	32 (31%)	19 (39%)	13 (24%)
Some college	51 (49.5%)	21 (43%)	30 (55%)
Unknown	3 (3%)	1 (2%)	2 (4%)

Table 1.2. Participants Who Received Public Aid as Adults

	All	Men	Women
Received	27 (26%)	7	20
Didn't receive	76 (74%)	42	34

Table 1.3. Participants' Work Histories

Type of work	All	% of Jobs	Men	Women
Auto (GM, auto store, Ford, auto detail)	6	6	6	0
Barber	1	1	1	0
Child care	3	3	0	3
City services (meter reader)	1	1	0	1
Construction	3	3	3	0
Education (project facilitator, teacher aide)	2	2	1	1
Financial services (financial planning, bank teller)	1	1	1	0
Food (fast food, grocery cook)	14	14	7	7
Health care (nurse aide, patient care)	13	13	3	10
Janitorial (housekeeping, custodians)	11	11	6	5
Manufacturing (assembly line, welding)	3	3	1	2
Odd jobs/temp work	2	2	2	0
Office (clerical, administrative assistant, receptionist)	14	14	3	11
Operations	8	8	0	8
Retail (clerk, customer service, store clerk, cashier)	12	12	1	11

Type of work	All	% of Jobs	Men	Women
Transportation and warehouses (truck loading, van driver)	3	3	2	1
Underground economy	1	1	1	0

Note: A total of 99 types of jobs were held by the 96 individuals with work histories.

Table 1.4. Number of Jobs Held by Participants as Adults

Number of jobs	All	Men	Women
3	13 (12.6%)	4	9
2	40 (38.8%)	21	19
1	43 (41.7%)	18	25
0	7 (6.7%)	6	1

Table 1.5. Participants Who Reported Having Been Incarcerated

All	Men	Women
8	7 of 49 (14%)	2 of 54 (3.7%)

What I sought to explore about Ypsilanti and its African American residents came to me through getting haircuts at Rammos, getting take-out fried chicken from the place just south of downtown, and making visits to various public housing developments and social service agencies. These and other encounters served as my mental springboard for making sense of black Ypsilantians. In committing to a full-fledged study in Ypsilanti, the resulting book became my effort to tell a story about African Americans whose experiences are similar to so many others in urban America. Yet as residents of a small city, they encounter uniqueness and particularities that posit some crucial differences to those encountered in larger cities. Lacking the intense concentration of people that is associated with the high-rise experience of larger-city urban poverty, low-income black Americans in Ypsilanti experience less congestion and are less easily hidden from their neighbors in other parts of town, because those other parts are often no more than a walk away from where they reside. The remaining chapters in part I explore in greater detail how black Ypsilantians live in a place powerfully affected by a single industry and struggling to contend with a newly emerging one.

NOTES

1. All references to the ages of the people in this book pertain to how old they were at the time of their first interviews for this project (which took place between 1999 and 2004).

2. Inkster is a city approximately 20 miles west of Detroit and 20 miles northeast of Ypsilanti. Inkster's economic and quality of life standing is similar to Ypsilanti's, and like the latter, it served as a bedroom community for the automobile industry as it blossomed throughout the twentieth century. The 2000 census reported a population of 30,115 people. The racial makeup of the city was 67.51% African American and 28.7% white American. The median annual household income was $35,950, and the median annual family income was $41,176. About 15.2% of families and 19.5% of the population lived below the poverty line, including 28.8% of those under age 18 and 13.4% of those age 65 or over (American Fact Finder 2010).

3. A notable exception is John Hartigan Jr.'s *Racial Situations: Class Predicaments of Whiteness in Detroit* (1999). This is an ethnographic study of three predominantly Caucasian communities in that city. As evident in the title, however, the African American experience is a pervasive but not central concern for that work. A more recent work, *Getting Ghost: Two Young Lives and the Struggle for the Soul of an American City*, by Luke Bergmann (2008), does provide a rich ethnographic portrait of two black males (and the tribulations they face as lower-level narcotics dealers) in that city. Consequently, it may stand as the only modern ethnographic study of African Americans in Detroit.

4. The notion of institutional ghetto employed here is drawn from the work of Horace Cayton and St. Claire Drake, who described the south side of Chicago as such a place in their classic study, *Black Metropolis: A Study of Negro Life in a Northern City* (1993 [1945]).

5. Willow Run is a small community located immediately northeast of Ypsilanti, yet the small size of both Willow Run and Ypsilanti often result in references to both as being part of the same community (in fact, the Willow Run school district merged with Ypsilanti's in 2013, further cementing the notion of a single community). Willow Run was created in the 1940s by the Federal Public Housing Administration to provide housing and easy access to the newly developed Ford Motor Company plant established there during that time. Thousands of units of housing for over 15,000 people were eventually constructed over about 2,600 acres of land (running just north of Michigan Avenue for about two miles to Geddes Road, and east of Prospect Road, near the eastern edge of Ypsilanti, for about a mile east to Ridge Road). This made the population of Willow Run about as large as that of Ypsilanti for much of the mid-twentieth century. The story of the founding of Willow Run is told in Carr and Stermer (1952) and Wilson (1956).

6. http://www.cityofypsilanti.com/Portals/0/docs/Planning/Master%20Plan/ypsimp_ch2background.pdf.

7. http://www.cityofypsilanti.com/Portals/0/docs/Planning/Master%20Plan/ypsimp_ch2background.pdf.

8. The transformations occurring in the decades immediately before and after the turn of the twenty-first century took place in what was a Democratic-leaning city throughout that time. Ypsilanti has promoted itself as one of the most tolerant and progressive communities in the state of Michigan. In the 1990s Ypsilanti became the first city in Michigan to pass a living wage ordinance. Its reputation for tolerance grew in the late 1990s, when the city adopted an ordinance to ban discrimination in housing, employment, and public accommodations on the basis of sexual orientation, gender identity/transgender status, race, body weight (i.e., being obese or underweight), religious affiliation, and country of origin, among several other categories. Although two ballot measures to repeal the ordinance were launched, one in 1998 and the other in 2002, both failed.

9. Chamber of Commerce, 1996, http://shapeypsi.com/assets/adopted-master-plan.pdf, 27.

10. In the ACS, health-care education services and health-care services appear as one category.

11. http://shapeypsi.com/assets/adopted-master-plan.pdf.

12. http://www.cityofypsilanti.com/Portals/0/docs/Planning/Master%20Plan/ypsimp_ch2background.pdf.

13. Index crimes are the eight crimes the FBI combines to produce its annual crime index. The index is calculated by dividing the reported crimes by the population, then multiplying the result by 100,000. This figure allows comparison of criminal occurrences across cities and regions of different size.

14. In a dissertation that details the contrast between Ann Arbor and Ypsilanti in local economies and consumer culture, anthropologist Kimberly Clum (2008) tells a story of how a supermarket chain built a grocery store in Ypsilanti that catered to the cultural tastes and preferences of many low-income African Americans, but it was physically constructed in extreme contrast to the Ann Arbor–based branches, which had painted murals and a more luxurious design. The Ann Arbor store also stocked gourmet items among a regular selection of groceries. The Ypsilanti store was built according to a basic warehouse design and stocked large quantities of items wholesaled by a generic low-cost distributer and placed alongside pig's feet, intestines, neck bones, and other items traditionally consumed in African American households.

Clum (2008, 63–64) argues the following:

> The commercial entities fostered by the relative economic boom in Ann Arbor similarly economically disenfranchise those with lower-incomes. Commercial entities develop in line with the consumptive needs and desires of a population (or, at least, with the perceptions of these). As Ann Arbor continues to draw highly educated, higher income residents to it, the kinds of stores, venues, and services that emerge are increasingly targeted to what might be considered bourgeois customers. Ann Arbor is full of businesses that cater to a well-educated population with significant disposable income: bookstores, restaurants, cafes, hair salons, spas, wine stores, gourmet food stores, expensive clothing stores, and art galleries.
>
> The cumulative effect of these differences has created a relatively dramatic polarization between the two towns in employment, housing, and commerce. Most of the better paying jobs are in Ann Arbor, while almost all of the lower-priced housing is in Ypsilanti. And virtually all of the high-end commercial outlets are in Ann Arbor while most of the low-cost venues

are in Ypsilanti (or, on the borders of Ann Arbor). As a result, where residents work, live, shop, and spend leisure time is significantly segregated between Ann Arbor and Ypsilanti by class and (due to the ways in which class in the United States is racialized) by race. For two towns so physically meshed together, the extent of social and spatial segregation between the populations is striking.

15. I am telling this story about black Ypsilantians now rather than closer to the time of my fieldwork because professional obligations in my career pulled me away from research. I spent nearly a decade chairing an academic department. This meant that aside from a book chapter that introduced some of my thinking about black Ypsilantians (Young 2008), there was no time for me to analyze or offer more about them. While spending seven years as an academic administrator, I continued to engage the city as well as several of the people featured in this book. As the tables in this chapter demonstrate, the lag in time has not resulted in significant change in the plight of black Ypsilantians. Hence, this account tells of a time in the recent past that resembles the present, particularly the issues and troubles that continue to challenge small-city black Americans today.

16. Michigan Works! partners with community organizations to meet the diverse needs of all customers. The Michigan Works! Association is a nonprofit membership organization that supports Michigan's talent development system, providing the following services: advocacy and participation in the legislative process by advancing and defending interests on the behalf of the Michigan Works! System, convening meetings as a way for members to network and share best practices, and holding events to promote the Michigan Works! System.

17. Numbers obtained using financial calculators at https://www.dollartimes.com/.

TWO

On the Doorstep of Ann Arbor and in the Shadow of Detroit

> If somebody come in here that we don't know, you gonna know about it. . . . And they don't let too many people bother each other, you know. Even though it's a lot of stuff [going on], I don't hear that [outsiders causing trouble] happening. It's real close as far as, you know, getting along. People looking out for each other. A lot of people get here and they get comfortable with the rent, and they get comfortable with, you know, because in the "hood" everybody close. . . . And they don't understand that this is a stepping stone. You step in, you step your ass out. Because it's nowhere for kids to live at all. You know. So some people just get comfortable. Some people may feel like they can't get out. You know what I mean? They stay forever. (Karen Andrews)

Karen is 25 years old and has been a resident of Ypsilanti her entire life. She has never lived beyond walking distance from where she was raised and has lived on the same city block for the past 18 years. Someone like her might see plenty of people come and go over that time. In fact, she has seen many families come to, but not really go very far from, her neighborhood. Even the fathers of some of the children in her neighborhood did not really go anywhere as much as they did not come around enough to be a part of the intimate lives of their children. Instead, many of those men came up in—and years later happen to still be somewhere around—Ypsilanti. At the time that she was interviewed, Karen was living with her boyfriend and three children (two boys, aged eight and seven, and a four-year-old girl).[1] All of her children had resulted from involvements with men prior to her current boyfriend. However, as her boyfriend resided with her and helped her provide for her three children, her household functioned much like a two-parent one.

Karen was raised in Ypsilanti by her two parents. Her father was a porter for much of his adult life, and her mother was a floor manager at a short-order restaurant for much of hers. Her parents experienced bouts of unemployment, which resulted in the family having to rely on public assistance at various points throughout Karen's upbringing. She has three brothers, and of the four of them she is the only one who has attended some college (she enrolled in a few computer training courses at Washtenaw County Community College). She withdrew from college to care for her children. Her boyfriend is a high school graduate who works as a laborer. At the time of her interview Karen was working as a machine operator for a book-binding company. In her past she had held one other job, serving as a cashier at a donut shop.

For some of Karen's neighbors, the absence of highly valued work, especially the blue-collar kind that was the trademark preference for Ypsilanti residents, left them with little hope for a better life and little knowledge of how to achieve one. Karen explained:

> Anybody can get out. . . . All it takes is a job, you know. . . . Well, not any job. You can't have any job, but some job is better than no job. But what it takes is we gotta get our child care issues together. We gotta be able to get a job that's gonna, even starting here, you know, a job that's gonna get you a little extra money so that you can start saving. Then we gotta get us a car. And then we're gonna look for a better job, maybe somethin' and then we can save for one or two classes.

As indicated in her remarks at the beginning of the chapter, Karen believed that her neighbors were comfortable with living in social circumstances that were quite familiar to them. According to her, the neighbors knew full well what kinds of conditions and challenges they faced in the neighborhood, and that they had the means to handle at least some of them (e.g., paying the rent and putting food on the table). They also had the comfort of knowing who else was in their social space, at least much of the time, and what those people were capable of doing. Thus, this kind of habituation brought forth at least some measure of security and stability even if the situation may appear to outsiders to be anything but secure and stable.

According to Karen, familiarity with their community bred a parochial mentality among her neighbors. That parochialism exacerbated their inability to achieve better life situations because what they saw in their immediate surroundings constituted most of what they imagined as accessible for themselves. The neighborhood had its problems, and these were not unlike the kind found in any low-income community. Karen shared her views about her neighborhood:

> It's not the people here, it's just the environment itself. The people that come. Because most of the people who shoot, who sell dope, who gamble they don't live here. Okay? But they come here because they ain't gonna do it [make trouble] at they momma house. And you gotta remember, this is the "hood." It's been like this. It ain't just started this year. It's been here for years and years and years. People have always came and stopped and did they thing. So it's just handed down from generation to generation.

For Karen, the sense of fatalism that penetrated life in the neighborhood around matters of socioeconomic mobility was also applicable to the ways in which people responded to crime and delinquency:

> Now we all sit here and we complain about this. We complain about that. But ain't nobody gain' go and do nothing because see they afraid of what's gone happen. You know, when you speak out, you get threw out. You know what I mean? And where else you gone go, you know, paying this much rent or whatever or on a limited budget, you know, when the average two-bedroom is five-six hundred, and the three-bedroom, don't even speak about houses. You know. What are you gonna do? So you keep your mouth shut. Hope it get better. If it don't, you still shut up.

Karen told of her neighborhood as a place where people not only knew each other but knew what to expect from each other. Consequently, it was easy for some people to desire to remain in place there because, despite the problems that come with living in a resource-depleted community, they had no capacity to think about accessing any other place. Like her neighbors, Karen knew much about the people on her block. Therefore, she spoke quite freely of how familiarity, even in the social turbulence and anxiety caused by life in poverty, breeds some level of comfort because those who experience this condition grow used to what they encounter. People like her also learn how to read and best respond to threats, such as violence, even if they cannot control when or how these occurrences unfold or what their ultimate outcome may be. The argument that outsiders are the source of many problems becomes the manner by which the unpredictability and capriciousness of life in disad-vantaged communities are addressed. That is, people in such environ-ments have no difficulty explaining what they understand about their local community. However, they also know that they often have little personal control of that space. Hence, that which is beyond their realm of control can be easily explained as resulting from outside influences.

Of course, what can be controlled by the residents is how, why, and what they choose to complain about to institutional authorities. Karen made clear that as a resident of public housing, too much complaining, or the wrong kind of it, could result in being put out of such housing by the authorities. Hence, while Ypsilanti may seem to have been a highly con-straining place for people like Karen, or for others a space filled with plenty of people who seemed to have plenty of problems, it also was a place of familiarity despite being so close to a city that on every measure appeared to be a much better place.

In order to provide a rich flavor of the kind of life situations experi-enced by black Ypsilantians, we turn here to a detailed account of the life experiences of several other residents. Carter Gaston, 28 years old, has been in Ypsilanti for just a few years. He was born in Detroit, where his mother and father raised him until they divorced when he was six years old. His father worked for Ford Motor Company and then became the director of a recreational center in the community. This enabled Carter and his sister to benefit from a comfortable early life. As a child Carter was able to bond with his father around sports. He recalled his father coaching youth baseball and basketball when Carter was very young and being by his dad's side during much of the activity. However, things changed when his parents divorced. Shortly after that occurrence, Carter explained, his father developed a drug addiction. His father began to withdraw from his son's life, leaving Carter with a mother who, as he believed, saw him as his father's son and a constant reminder of what was wrong with that man.

Carter ultimately did follow the pernicious path that his mother ex-pected of him. He was incarcerated by the age of 16 for shooting at a group of males he said were preparing to accost him at a party. He returned home, at the age of 22, after serving six years. He has moved around southeastern Michigan since then. Throughout that time he has had a conflictual relationship with his mother:

[We have] a love-hate relationship. She believes that I'm institutional-
ized and my mentality is that of a prisoner no matter what. Mind you,
like I have to constantly remind my mother, I went to prison when I
was 16. I went to college when I was in prison [without earning a
degree]. I had a life sentence. I represented myself on my appeal and I
won. After six years, I was acquitted in a new trial. You know, I don't
really know where she pulls a prison mentality out of that, but, none-
theless, that's my relationship with my parents. Basically, there isn't
one. They're still alive, but I don't communicate with my mother. My
father, I don't really know what state he's in. He comes back in town,
uh, probably every 90 days. I don't always get an opportunity to see
him, or even know that he's there for that matter. He tends to leave
before I'm even made aware of the fact that he's there. It's like that.

As he said, incarceration did not prevent Carter from pursuing his education. In fact, he said that he was committed to schooling prior to ever
going to jail, despite doing things that caused him trouble in school:

I've been to all the junior high schools in Detroit, and about seven high
schools. I've been kicked out of the Detroit public schools and been to
alternative schools. But, I'm a wizard, though. Everywhere they sent
me, I got As and Bs, so they didn't have no other choice but to put me
back into the system, you know what I mean?

Carter's early adulthood involved moving around among extended family members throughout southeastern Michigan. His oldest sister, who
was a few years younger than he, died soon after he was released from
prison. Carter left home soon thereafter. He lived with an aunt in Albion,
Michigan (a small town located in the south-central part of the state),
where he quickly came to see what small-town life for an adult was like.
Referring to Albion as a "hick town," he explained that he taught his
male cousins how to cut hair, thus preparing at least one of them to get a
license and find work in a barbershop. Otherwise, he worked odd jobs to
support whatever households took him in. He said that his aunt was like
many women in his family, who believed that it was the man's job to earn
the money:[2]

She's never worked a day in her life. She was raised by my grandmother who believes that you should have a man who is a country bumpkin
and will allow you to just sit on your ass basically, and do nothing. You
know, my grandmother was like that. My grandmother's been married
like seven times, to rich people, though, you know what I mean? Rich

people with problems, too. I mean, she was even married to a guy who was kind of retarded, but he was wealthy.

Carter learned to have a negative view of women because his life brought him into contact with so few who were good to him, and in his mind they were not really motivated to be good to themselves either:

> You know, my mother never did anything for me anyway. If it wasn't for my uncles, man, I wouldn't have had nothing when I was coming up, you know what I'm saying? If it wasn't for my uncles, period. You know, my uncles used to come over and look at my report card, man, and, you know, that was my thing, you know what I mean? I mean, if I can't do nothing else right, you know, I ain't no dummy, you know what I'm saying? I can get good grades, I can pay attention in school, that ain't nothing [for me to do]. I can read. As long as I can read, possibilities are infinite, you know what I mean? So, you know, I get my report card, my uncles come through, man, looking like a million bucks, you know, pull out paper bags full of money, man, and break me off [some money]. So, my report card, my mama didn't *even* do that, you know?

When asked about the behavior of the women in his family, Carter quickly said that his younger sister was a hard worker (she worked as a bank teller). He also said that he had an aunt who was a police officer and a few relatives who worked hard at good jobs "all over the state of Michigan"; he claimed that he had female cousins who were "between welfare and maxing out as topless dancers." The men were faring no better. As Carter stated:

> Guy cousins, man, they want to be drug dealers so bad. They bums, man. They ain't nowhere, man. Everybody in my family dies, man, you know, my cousins especially, you know. They all look to me to bring everybody out of the trenches, you know what I'm saying? I done saved them so many times. You know, like, when I came home from prison, man, they was out here starving, you know what I'm saying? I changed all that, you know, I came out here and made it easy for everybody, you know what I'm saying? I was really plugged when I got out of prison, you know what I mean? I had rubbed elbows with a few good people, I'll put it like that, you know.

Carter's past life has informed his present activities. He now fluctuates between the underground and aboveground economy while trying to maintain something of a stable home life:

> I'm married, now, you know what I mean? I've been married now for
> five years. Five of the six years that I've been home. I lived a bachelor
> lifestyle for the first four years of my marriage. And, uh, while I was
> living that bachelor lifestyle, I was hustling, too, real heavy, but I was
> also known as a hustler, as one who—I kept a job, too, and never made
> less than $14 an hour, you know what I mean? Even as a hustler, that
> was my reputation, you know what I'm saying? I've always worked,
> and I've always worked a good job, you know. Chrysler was the only
> manual labor job *I've ever* had. My whole work history is shirt-tie.

As for trying to help his extended family, Carter said, "I can't make y'all
look good and make y'all shine, because all y'all do is just screw me
anyway, you know, so I'm through with that. My life now is just all about
my wife and kid."

For Carter, family life means a combination of hustling, looking for
better work in the formal economy, dealing with an indictment that was
recently served on him, and living on a block in Ypsilanti filled with
people who seem to him to be pretty fast at going nowhere:

> Oh, my neighbors ain't have no jobs, man. It was too much money on
> our block. You got to know, those drug houses there, that money is—if
> it's in your neighborhood, it's [where the money is]. So, I guess people
> was just living off of each other, living off the earth, more or less. In my
> neighborhood, nobody went to work, man, everybody was home eve-
> ryday. You know, the only people that went anywhere, man, in the
> morning, was the kids, man. The kids went to school, man, you know
> what I mean? That was about it.

Carter told of his efforts to try to move up the right way in the world of
work, unlike some of his neighbors. He explained that he had worked as
a sales representative for various car dealers and clerked at various car
rental agencies since landing a job at a U-Haul shop shortly after being
released from prison. Jobs came and went for Carter as he let his entrepreneurial spirit, which rested on his propensity to get involved in hus-
tles of various sorts, push and pull him in different directions. This included his losing about as many jobs as he acquired.

Ypsilanti is where Carter finally came to settle as an adult and a married man. He finds that his life is a bit more controllable here because this
small town does not appear as challenging and troublesome as did his
hometown of Detroit. As he has seen rock bottom through his years in
prison, though, Carter is convinced that he can face the challenges in his
life and ultimately make a better way for himself. In explaining his worst

years, which was when he was in prison (and the only time he reported making less than $14.00 an hour), he said:

> I sweated rocks on top of rocks. . . . Cleaned toilets on top of toilets for $0.54 an hour for six years. You know what I'm saying? I got something against slave wages, really, though. You know what I mean? You know, for real. Not to mention where my intelligence for six years didn't do nothing for me. As a matter of fact, it worked against me. You know what I'm saying? Because I had a brain and I was putting it to use, I got treated like *even* less than a human being, you know what I'm saying? You treat a dummy better than you treat me. I get up and I go to school everyday. This clown out here playing basketball, this clown over here walking the yard with a lag, you know, with this nigger with lipstick on. . . . You know, I'm hitting the books everyday, and, you know, you [the prison officials] got a problem with me.

Despite his sense of efficacy, Carter has a melancholy vision of self. This was most evident when he was asked to reflect upon his life of rapid transition from job to job after being incarcerated for all of his late adolescence. In particular, when asked what he felt he had learned about himself from all of his jobs, he said, "That I can't keep one. That I can't keep one. I guess some of what my mother thinks about me is probably true, you know."

Carter's movement between formal employment and underground activity, and between what he believed were sometimes decent and sometimes far less than decent wages, is the kind of turbulent life history that is somewhat more extreme than but not wholly unlike the lives of the majority of the people featured in this book. Depending on the day of a given week, the week of a given month, or the month of a given year, he could either be unemployed or hard at work. At those times he could be providing consistently for his family or struggling to do so. In short, his life, like the others in this book, reflected a consistent pattern of inconsistency, and this is the case for the African American working poor in general (based in big and small cities).

Brian Fuller is also a young man with a troubled past. He was 26 when interviewed and has a general equivalency diploma (GED) acquired while he was in prison. He and his fiancée care for two daughters. One, aged two, is the product of his fiancée's relationship with another partner. The second, who is two months old, is his and his fiancée's biological daughter. Brian was raised by his mother and grew up in Ypsilanti. She worked for temporary employment agencies doing menial labor when she was not receiving public assistance. Brian did not know much about his father. He explained that his father was abusive toward him and his two sisters (all of whom have different fathers) while growing up. As Brian's father was incarcerated for lengthy periods of time, he was not a consistent presence in the household. In fact, his presence was so minimal that Brian could not recall anything about his father's employment history or schooling, or even his age.

Brian has served five years in a juvenile detention center for stealing an automobile. He also reported that he had sold drugs in his past. In talking about his turbulent personal history, he said, "I felt like I had to do things for myself. . . . As I got older, I felt like I never really got a chance to be a child . . . like most kids who normally get a chance to do. . . . At ten [I was doing things] I shouldn't have even been thinking about, you know."

Brian made parole in March 2001 and got engaged shortly after he was released. In 2002 he strove to stabilize his work situation so that he could be a good father to his daughters. He found work through a temporary employment agency that placed him with a landscaping company. He was interviewed for this project when he was two months into his employment with the company. Since his parole he also has worked as a dietary aid for a health-care service center.

Although finding better and more secure employment was a priority for him, so was the effort to keep his family together, as child protective services was investigating his fiancée and him for negligence after their youngest daughter was accidentally burned with hot water by the oldest. Brian explained that the hot water in their small apartment was measured at 156 degrees, and that the older child had been running the water when she accidentally spilled some on her half sister. Determining that parental negligence had occurred, the court took their children out of the home. In the weeks prior to being interviewed, Brian and his fiancée were working on getting the children back home with them.

With his daughters not at home with him and his recent release from jail leaving him with an extraordinarily brief postrelease work history, Brian was in a most precarious situation. Brian did have a car, which put him in a position of privilege relative to many low-income individuals who seek employment. That car was his principal resource for getting to work and seeking out better work opportunities. However, he explained that he had to be very careful about how he went about finding work because he was not in possession of a valid driver's license. It had been suspended due to his inability to pay fines for violations that he had incurred. He and his fiancée also were behind in rent by about a thousand dollars, and this was a motivating factor as well for finding a better job. In assessing his current situation, he said, "I don't have any money, but I got a job, she's got a job, so we do have income coming in. . . . I got a friend that does landscaping, and I'm trying to work some with him."

The primary goal for Brian and his fiancée was getting their children back home and creating a positive household environment for the family. Accordingly, even though they were in extreme debt, Brian said that any additional work that his fiancée might find would have to end when the children came home. He believed that the cost of childcare would outweigh any income that her second job could accrue. As he said after being asked about childcare possibilities, "So, we can't afford a babysitter. . . . We're not even going to bother with that."

Brian's desire to get a permanent job and create a stable work history was initially mandated by the terms of his parole. Yet the crisis that came upon him with his children, coupled with the financial problems, forced him to determine that, at least for the short-term future, all of his energy had to be put into work, so that his fiancée could be the central presence at home once the children came back. In explaining how he thought about balancing his efforts concerning work with his interest in being a consistently visible father at home, he said:

> I might be a little more tired. But that's about it. . . . I kind of use it as motivation because I want my children to have more than I had. That's why, probably the reason I try to work and try to work more hours. One week I had worked like sixteen hours, three days in a row just so I could . . . this is before we had the youngest one, just so I could get her a little stuff for Christmas. I guess I want them to have more than I had. I just use it as motivation. I mean, and I want to try to get . . . do more things and get more things.

Brian has made the kind of commitment that men usually make when the household and the workplace serve as simultaneous sources of tension: He chose to commit to going to work. In his case, however, that choice was made without having the same degree of freedom available to more privileged people. Brian strongly believed that he had to demonstrate a capacity to be a consistent wage earner and a dependable employee, given his criminal record. He also had to resolve his debt in order for him and his fiancée to maintain a household. Consequently, Brian did not perceive that he had a choice in terms of reconfiguring the time division between work and home. For him, work would always have to get the attention.

Ellen Martin, age 23 and a high school graduate, was raised by her grandmother in Detroit. There was no male adult figure at home. Shortly after her mother gave birth to her, Ellen was literally dropped off on her grandmother's doorstep, who by that time was retired and sharing a household with her own sister, an employee with the Ford Motor Company. Ellen lives in Ypsilanti with her husband of eight years and their two daughters, ages two and one.

Up until nearly a month prior to her interview, Ellen worked as a food preparer for an adult care center. In the past five years she has worked as a cashier, security guard, and day-care staffer. Her husband was in a minimally skilled area of construction, making approximately $15.00 an hour. Up until a year before she was interviewed in 2002, Ellen and her husband were in a childless, two-income household. At that time they were experiencing a level of job security that escaped the other people featured in this book. However, in 1999 her husband had been severely injured in a shooting. Ellen reported that the hospital doctors discovered about 15 bullet holes in his body. Each of their children was born at some point in the midst of his long recovery from this injury. Consequently, the burden of support for the family fell solely on Ellen. She began rearing the children as well as tending to the medical and emotional needs of her husband, thus adding significantly to the normal pressures involved with caring for a family. As she explained:

> At first, we didn't have no kids. I had the kids the last two years. And, um, you know, we had gas in the car, rent paid up for the whole year, vacations, everything. But when we started having kids, that's when everything started going bad. He couldn't work no more. Um, I had to work—I had to work two jobs for my last child in order to maintain. We were living in Canton for, I would say, five years, and then we had to move to Ypsilanti the last year because we couldn't maintain the rent that we were. . . . He's unable [to work], so he'll just have to get Social Security or something like that to help out, though. He's working on that right now. They're [federal government services agencies] constantly denying him and I'm tired of that, you know because we have everything proved, that, you know, he got rods in his neck, he got bullets in him and he can't hold a job, you know, and they're giving us

a hard time. So, that'll be income right there [when he begins receiving government aid], but until then, he's helping out with the kids. He's doing what he can do, which is not much, but he's trying, so that's a good thing.

Ellen had given up her job a month prior to being interviewed because she had no support in caring for her children while her husband was recovering. At that time, she was in the midst of finding a job that would be closer to her home and would have some hourly flexibility.

Considering these four participants together, Karen Andrews has a life of little promise but of much consistency. Carter Gaston has one of self-professed promise but also of turbulence. Brian Fuller has a job but has encountered the same kind of social turbulence that has come Carter's way. Ellen had a life of great stability until a health crisis occurred that left her family in an impending financial crisis as well. While neither Karen, Carter, Brian, nor Ellen described having an ideal work situation, all were employed and were used to having jobs as adults. Each also lived in a relatively stable, but certainly not tension-free, household situation. Aside from these similarities, their life histories and current situations show contrasts. Carter and Ellen are experienced workers who come from slightly more privileged backgrounds than Karen and Brian, although Ellen had recently fallen down the socioeconomic ladder due to a family crisis. Karen and Brian are from much more humble backgrounds. However, while Karen has maintained some connection to work as an adult, Brian has encountered some trouble with the law. The tensions at home have surfaced around trying to keep immediate family members in the household (Brian) or balancing employment responsibilities with the desire to find and spend more quality time with children (Karen, Carter, and Ellen). Hence, each is struggling with navigating the work-family divide when neither work nor family brings them the kind of emotional or material security that Americans generally desire from each setting.

These four participants represent the range of work and family experiences of the people featured in this book. At different points in their lives they have fallen along the continuum of the unemployed to the working poor. Some of their struggle has been about finding the kind of work that would allow them to achieve economic security and emotional well-being (and this struggle certainly is not unique to low-income African

Americans in a small city like Ypsilanti). Some of it involves efforts to erase the effects of personal historical experiences that have marked them as less-than-deserving people in the eyes of potential employers (again, a situation that is not unique to disadvantaged residents of Ypsilanti). Otherwise, some of the struggle emerges from their believing that the people around them, family and neighbors, cannot or will not get ahead, or that they otherwise let the forces and conditions of the community they live in keep them grounded in a place that is highly unsatisfying.

It seems that their stories could come from disadvantaged African Americans in any large city in the United States. The fact that they could, however, is not the point of telling these stories. Instead, a striking feature about these people is that the stories they tell, about themselves and their communities, take place in an area that is a short drive or bus ride to what many would presume to be a better environment. They live less than a few miles from Ann Arbor, but like the great majority of the people in this book, they do not much discuss whether or how that city might afford them better opportunities. More is said in the next section of this chapter about their and others' reactions to Ann Arbor. However, in order to more fully understand the limits of their future-oriented thinking, we remain focused a bit longer on how they consider their immediate communities.

Like many black Ypsilantians, these people make clear that a lot is going on for them in Ypsilanti. What is going on, however, is cause for concern and stress rather than informing them about how to pursue opportunity. Equally important, they all demonstrate that even a small place can make a big difference in how they take stock of their life situations and prospects. Like many of their neighbors, friends, and associates discussed in the following pages, they draw significant distinctions between the small city they live in and the small city next door to them. The references to that other small city help convey how they position themselves in the social world and what this means for understanding how disadvantage is experienced for low-income African Americans in a small town. As I further explore, this is only a part of the story of how they live on the edge. (Detroit looms large in other ways that are treated later on in this book.)

ON THE DOORSTEP OF ANN ARBOR

In a geographical sense, Ypsilanti is much closer to its more privileged neighbor, Ann Arbor, than it is to Detroit. However, proximity does not breed similarity. Ypsilanti's measures of educational and economic achievement fall short of Ann Arbor's. A 2014 Ypsilanti-Ann Arbor comparison is shown in table 2.1. Ypsilanti is a bedroom community for residents who work in Ann Arbor and, to a far lesser extent, for those who work in places east of the city (including Detroit). Therefore, if promise and possibility exist for the struggling residents of Ypsilanti, it is conceivable that Ann Arbor would be the site where both could unfold for them. The orientation of many of Ypsilanti's low-income black Americans, however, is that Ann Arbor is a foreign terrain. As they explained, people like themselves—African Americans of working-class status or below—were not often comfortable in that city.

Pauline Hamilton, age 21, was single and had no children when she was interviewed. She had no job as well, despite having taken some classes in community college over a few years. In her recent past she had worked in customer service, and she was now focused on trying to get back to school in order to help her find work. As she explained, whatever

Table 2.1.   Comparative Demographic Profile—Ypsilanti and Ann Arbor

		Ypsilanti Population 19,569	Ann Arbor Population 117,700
Race	Hispanic and Latino	3.9%	4.1%
	Two races	4.3%	3.6%
	Asian	3.4%	14.4%
	American Indian and Alaska Native	0.6%	0.3%
	Black	29.2%	7.7%
	White	61.5%	73.0%
Education	HS graduate or higher	89.9%	96.4%
	BA or higher	36.0%	70.9%
Income	Median household income	$32,148	$56,835
	Per capita income in past 12 months	$21,801	$36,074

Source: Marsh 2016.

she was trying to do did not involve trying to put Ann Arbor into play as a site for her own future possibilities:

> I don't interact with them [Ann Arbor residents] very well at all and I get into confrontations, whereas I can relate more to people in lower poverty. That's where I live at is lower poverty, and I interact with them and am more approachable, whereas I get flustered if I went into an interview with them [more privileged people], because, like I said, that's why I'm taking that communication class, because I feel inferior to them for some reason. I always think that they're probably looking at my address.

The belief that Ann Arbor residents look down on black Americans from Ypsilanti was quite rampant in the minds of many of the Ypsilanti residents featured in this book. For nearly half of them, despite being close to home, Ann Arbor was not at all close to them. Instead, they felt neglected and disrespected. As they reported that they did not often visit Ann Arbor, their specific moments of conflict and tension while there loomed large in their readings of what that city had to offer them. More important, they felt that there were many other communities in southeastern Michigan that were more appropriate for people like them. In expressing sentiments that are commonly held by lower-income African Americans when asked to reflect on how much they are positively or appropriately regarded by the more privileged, they often said that they felt like they were invisible.

For example, Carmen Granderson is a 22-year-old who is much like Pauline. Carmen also has no children, no spouse, and no current job. She attended college for a short period of time. She reported that she worked as an airline agent but left her job due to a pregnancy that ultimately was unsuccessful, and the only other job she had had in her life was as a retail cashier. She told the following story about why Ann Arbor is not the kind of place that made her feel comfortable:

> I don't care what nobody says. Ann Arbor is one of the most prejudiced cities. Other than like Howell, Michigan [a city west of Ann Arbor that was reputed to be home to a Ku Klux Klan activist who died in 1992].[3] Because it's a college town on top of that. . . . You could be going to the University of Michigan and they still . . . you walk into a store and they still just treat you different. Like they watching you, like acting like they're not watching but they're watching you, and it's like you can. . . . I'm not going to steal anything. I'm about [to] pay for it. . . . They are very prejudiced.

Carmen supported her opinion by describing how she had entered a restaurant in Ann Arbor and was not greeted properly by the hostess:

> I went in there and I'm sitting there, you know, waiting. I'm standing there like waiting for the lady to say, "How many?" And she just was talking to her friend. I'm just standing there. I'm like, "Hello," you know. But I wasn't rude. I'm standing there. And then like this other couple walks . . . an older white couple, they walk in and she was like, "Two?" I'm like, "Wait!" I was just like, "Hold on, wait, wait. Four, please, non-smoking." And she was like, "Oh, I didn't know you were waiting." She says she didn't know we were waiting on somebody [but she] didn't ask.

Stories of being made to feel inadequate and neglected were common themes in how some of these people spoke about Ann Arbor. Accordingly, their sense of comfortable space was centered on areas that appeared to be better for black Americans. Even if such occurrences might have solely been due to race, these individuals consistently stated that their being from Ypsilanti made them unacceptable in Ann Arbor.

Walter Washington was 32 years old when interviewed. He has a GED, is married with two children, and works as a machine operator. As he put it, "Because Ann Arbor is predominantly white, so you might have a more difficult time simply because of the favoritism thing kicking in. So I might be better off in Detroit or Inkster where there's more populated blacks and they're used to seeing blacks."

In contrast to Ann Arbor, Detroit was a common point of reference as a place that was more understandable to black Ypsilantians. The very existence of a large city that was considered a more comfortable space for black Americans created a clear and visible comparative context for talking about Ann Arbor. Hence, it is not surprising that so many Ypsilanti residents would make strong distinctions. In doing so, they could firmly describe Ann Arbor as a "white" space in comparison to Ypsilanti, Inkster, or Detroit. In doing so, that white space became the imagined if not actual site of threat, discomfort, and unfamiliarity to black Ypsilantians.

IN THE SHADOW OF DETROIT

Detroit offers an urban experience far beyond anything found in Ypsilanti. The size and history of Detroit make it an important point of reference for black Ypsilantians as they talk about the world of work and work opportunity. What lingers for these residents is that Detroit was the model city for industry, especially for black Americans who sought opportunities in that sector. Throughout much of the twentieth century, Detroit was the city that worked, and it worked in ways that paralleled how Ypsilanti worked, largely because Detroit's growth in the industrial era spawned that which took place throughout southeastern Michigan, including Ypsilanti.

In ways that are not as virtuous, Detroit also appeared to be a larger-scale version of what Ypsilanti is for African Americans. That is, by the end of the twentieth century it became a city where African Americans struggled to survive economic decline and the social ills associated with it. Detroit has borne the burden of being regarded as a troubled city for African Americans. From 1980 to 2000 it lost almost 300,000 residents. It lost another 200,000 between 2000 and 2010. This was mostly due to white flight, although the entire population of Detroit has experienced a rapid decline since the dawn of the twenty-first century (Seelye 2011).

Ypsilanti certainly does not reflect the magnitude of some of the social problems affecting its larger neighbor, but by drawing comparisons to Detroit, it becomes clear that Ypsilanti has suffered from the same afflictions and maladies on a scale that is concerning for a city of its size. An Ypsilanti-Detroit crime comparison provides an example (see tables 2.2 and 2.3).

Despite its significant problems, Detroit offers the image of how a large city did effectively operate once upon a time. As such, it lingered in the minds of black Ypsilantians when they were asked to talk about what possibility and opportunity could look like for people like themselves.

Table 2.2. Comparative Crime Statistics, Ypsilanti, Detroit, United States, 2006

Crimes per 10,000 population	Ypsilanti, MI	Detroit, MI	National
Murder	1.84	4.7	0.7
Forcible rape	5.98	6.7	3.2
Robbery	34.9	81.8	20.6
Aggravated assault	84.9	148.6	33.6
Burglary	163.9	205.0	81.3
Larceny theft	373.3	240.7	260.2
Vehicle theft	57.9	259.1	50.2

Source: AreaConnect 2006.

Table 2.3. **Comparative Crime Measures, Ypsilanti, Detroit, United States, 2016**

Crimes per 10,000 population	Ypsilanti, MI	Detroit, MI	National
Murder	0.0	4.5	0.5
Forcible rape	15.5	8.7	4.0
Robbery	21.4	43.8	10.3
Aggravated assault	45.2	147.9	24.9
Burglary	54.7	130.06	46.9
Larceny theft	250.7	208.4	174.5
Vehicle theft	21.4	133.1	23.7

Source: NeighborhoodScout 2016.

One of the most direct responses about Detroit came from Carmen Granderson:

> I'm not going to lie. Mostly good jobs are toward Detroit. You know, the good paying job with benefits and stuff like that. Because around here like my one friend, she's been working at Wendy's for like four years, and Wendy's doesn't offer any medical benefits, no kind of 401K, nothing. Like *you've* been working there for four years and it's like you're not going anywhere. She hasn't *even* got a raise.

Ypsilanti serves as more than a geographic space between Detroit and Ann Arbor. It is also a liminal space. That is, it represents a divide in the kinds of racial experiences that black Ypsilantians report having, and this affects how they think about familiar and comfortable places. Detroit represents a certain kind of special place for them because it is the closest part of the America that reflects a once upon a time image of black American socioeconomic success. Hence, Detroit is familiar not because it is geographically close to black Ypsilantians, but because it is symbolically proximate.

Marvin Morris is 29 years old and the father of three children. He served in the US Navy after completing high school. After being honorably discharged, he returned to Ypsilanti and worked in patient care for a heath-care agency and as a store clerk (the latter being the job he had when interviewed). His having seen some of the world outside of Ypsilanti has provided him with a broader perspective than many black Ypsilantians have for thinking about the location of good work opportunities. Nevertheless, he stated his attitude quite succinctly (and much like Walter Washington, whom we heard from earlier): "They would be more prone to give me a chance [at finding work] if I was in, you know, Detroit."

As was the case for many black Ypsilantians, Detroit seemed like a place that was right for black Americans who aspired to find work. Familiarity with that city often came from having contact with relatives who were raised there or who lived there at some point in their lives.

Sherry Lewis, a 24-year-old custodian at the University of Michigan who did not finish high school said:

> Everybody in my family, from my grandmother to my aunt to my mom, my uncles, none of them I've known not to work, and they've all had good jobs. My aunt, she had good jobs. She was an alcoholic, and she worked at like Kroger's and stuff, but them are good jobs, you know. And, she was a good cook. But, then my uncle that lives in Detroit, he been working for this auto parts place ever since I was a little girl and now he like owns the store. Then my other uncle, he worked for the city, I don't know exactly what he did, but he did stuff around the city. . . . My uncle in Detroit, his wife, she was working for Blue Cross Blue Shield.

Detroit's value for many black Ypsilantians was not rooted in any strong desire to relocate to that city. Nor did it necessarily have to do with their having spent extensive amounts of time there. This was made evident by the inability of many black Ypsilantians to say exactly where they would find work in that city and exactly how they could find a better life there. Some black Ypsilantians talked about relatives who had lived in Detroit or continued to do so. This tenuous connection that the larger city enabled them to draw from stories told to them by their relatives facilitated their own imaginings of the utility Detroit might have for them. That city could be imagined as whatever black Ypsilantians might want it to be, because they did not have to build such conceptions from sustained and intimate exposure to it. Of course a boundary on that imagination was the common knowledge that Ypsilanti's history as a thriving automobile town rested on Detroit as the metropolis that was central to this development. Hence, without having to venture into that city or to know with any great precision what kinds of work might be there contemporarily, Detroit served as a symbolic reference to the kinds of work opportunity in southeastern Michigan that were familiar and appealing to black Ypsilantians. It became an effective point of reference for thinking about new and better opportunities. This is why Detroit mattered for people who did not necessarily frequent it, and why it mattered in ways that contrasted with their views about Ann Arbor, the city that was much closer and more easy to encounter.

SOCIOECONOMIC DISADVANTAGE IN A NEW VEIN

The small-city experience of African Americans in Ypsilanti is nested within their encounters with Ann Arbor and their sensibilities about southeastern Michigan and its staple city, Detroit. This situation provides a unique spin on some of the conceptual language used to study the African American urban poor. Two concepts used to explain how being physically located in a place affects the social opportunities and possibilities for such people are *social isolation* and *concentration effects*. These terms were given great effect by the work of sociologist William Julius Wilson (1987). He argued that social isolation resulted from a lack of contact or sustained interaction with individuals or institutions that reflect socioeconomic success and stability. It is a condition of extreme physical and social distance between residents of chronically impoverished urban communities and the more privileged spaces that stand miles apart from them or, if nearby, are separated by way of highways, railroad tracks, or other physical structures (Wilson 1987).

The implication of social isolation is that living in such a condition leads to the inability to participate in and benefit from the accoutrements of mainstream life and culture (Harrell and Peterson 1992; Jencks and Peterson 1991; Massey and Denton 1993). That kind of living has also been argued to lead to the generation of behavior not conducive to developing good work histories. This is so especially because social isolation places those subjected to it as disconnected from communities of people whose everyday life experiences are organized around work. The effects of saturation in social networks and social exposure with little other than chronically poor people were thereafter understood to be a vital structural condition of life in poverty. Accordingly, the introduction of this concept into sociological analysis created an analytical space for assessing the effects of an enduring lack of social and geographic connection between the urban poor and more affluent people.

Concentration effects, the second concept advanced by Wilson (1987) that became central to modern urban poverty research, refers to the social outcomes resulting from large numbers of impoverished people living in proximity to each other. In short, the increase of socioeconomically disadvantaged people residing within a defined geographic space results in a saturation of exposure to the social malaise that accompanies disadvantage. By way of comparison, think of the situation of economically disadvantaged individuals and families who may reside near people of greater socioeconomic means. In the latter case, the disadvantaged may be shunned or not fully invited into the social spheres of the more privileged, but by virtue of proximity they may be exposed to ideas, information, and resources (such as community organizations, well-resourced public libraries, and benevolent or well-resourced individuals) that can benefit them.

Given the application of these terms in the recent history of urban poverty research, one can think of social isolation and concentration effects as properties of life in disadvantaged, large-city neighborhoods. However, the case of Ypsilanti allows for a nuanced consideration of social isolation and poverty concentration that is specifically applicable to the small-city context. Karen Andrews's remarks about the people in her community, presented at the beginning of this chapter, call attention to the way social isolation becomes manifested for many low-income African Americans in Ypsilanti in a unique small-city way. That is, struggling black Ypsilantians encounter neither social isolation nor concentration effects to anywhere near the degree struggling African Americans who reside in large cities do. However, they suffer from being isolated from a thriving sphere of postindustrial success and being concentrated in a sphere of industrial decline.

CONCLUSION

The American creed of upward mobility rests on a series of assumptions and expectations. One is that a job should deliver an income that allows for the consistent provision of food and housing for oneself and one's family. That creed includes the notion that a home should provide a space for emotional comfort and security (Bartlett and Steele 2012; Johnson 2014; Putnam 2007; Moen and Roehling 2005). Most important, it includes the notion that a job should allow for socioeconomic security, if not prosperity, home and car ownership, the prospect of securing college education for children, and an income that provides support for retirement. Throughout the middle of the twentieth century many blue-collar jobs in America delivered on at least some of these expectations. White-collar work delivered on even more of them. The American Dream is elusive for the people in this book. Accordingly, like many of the working poor, black Ypsilantians are more concerned with immediate financial needs and finding jobs that provide stability if not other elements of the American Dream. They want consistent income and the feeling that life can get better over time. They want employment that will enable them to give their children a stronger start in life than they had and that will result in their children surpassing their own socioeconomic status. What they want is that which seems to be well in hand for many of the families that live in neighboring Ann Arbor.

There is no extreme geographic isolation for black Ypsilantians. They live quite close to a small city of relative privilege and comfort. Even though Ypsilanti is a small city, it is easy for residents to come away from their experiences there with little understanding of what else or what more there is to life in other places, especially those other places that are as close as is the more affluent Ann Arbor. Theirs is a special case of social isolation, to the extent that they feel strongly disconnected from Ann Arbor, but it is the geographic proximity that fuels their clear sense of social disconnection. For black Ypsilantians, then, the emotional and cognitive distance from Ann Arbor overrides their geographical proximity to it, thus allowing for a cognitive isolation to emerge. Physical space itself is not the only meaningful feature in isolation. What is geographically close by is not embraced as familiar. Intriguingly, geographic isolation does exist for them in the case of Detroit and other parts of southeastern Michigan. While they do not experience consistent engagement with the city and the border region, the pull in that direction has a bit to do with how race is read into those spaces, but more so with how familiar kinds of employment opportunities have been.

Low-income residents of Ypsilanti are not always visibly hidden from, nor do they lack some means of exposure to, those with more socioeconomic privilege (and who happen to be mostly white Americans). Instead, life in despair in this small city has meant that the African Americans who have been subjected to this environment experience a cognitive isolation that overrides the geographic proximity that they have to more privileged communities and people.

Accordingly, and as explored in the following chapters, this isolation matters not simply for how black Ypsilantians feel about Ann Arbor, but also for how they remain distant from their immersion in and understanding of the postindustrial environment that shapes the contemporary world of work. The business of the next chapter is to explore how they do so in regard to perceptions of work and work opportunity and the rationale for how those perceptions sometimes involve focusing on Detroit when discussing why they see work opportunity as they do.

NOTES

1. Any reference to time in this chapter takes the year of the interview for each person as the contemporary moment. Thus, Karen "has lived" on that block from 1972 through 2000.

2. A body of literature in the sociology of occupations and the study of work-family balances has affirmed how much men seem to find more comfort in work than at home (Hochschild 1997; Kanter 1977; Nelson and Smith 1999; Townsend 2002).

3. The reputation of this activist, Robert E. Miles, was heightened by reported public cross burnings while he was alive on farmland property that he owned near Howell and the discovery and subsequent auctioning off of Klan memorabilia found in his possession upon his death in 1992 (see Peters 2005).

THREE

Experiencing the World of Work in a City on the Edge

It is so easy to find a job nowadays. You could walk out the door and people will just say, "What are you doing, man? You want to work?" You can find it. It may not be the job you want [but] I can walk to a fast food restaurant and say, "Hey, how you doing, blah, blah, blah, my name is Carl. You know, I'm looking for some part time work." "What do you want to do?" "Just wash the dishes." "Ok." See you can find a job. Jobs are plentiful out there right now. (Carl Fulton)

Really nothing [is available in terms of work opportunity], sales jobs, telemarketing jobs, the ones I was applying for; daycare jobs, but no career, you know what I'm saying? You can't carry it on for the rest of your life. You can't get nowhere. (Ellen Martin)

You know, if a person really wants to work, there are plenty of jobs out here. Plenty. It may not be what you want, but there are plenty, plenty jobs. You know, I never did buy that old saying about, you know, "I just can't find a job. I can't find a job." I was always able to find work. Always. I've never been out looking for a job and couldn't find one. A lot of times it wasn't what I wanted but it was an honest living. It was work. So to me it's not hard at all, you know, especially in our area. (Jessica Boyd)

These comments capture the general frame of thinking of black Ypsilantians about work and work opportunity. When interviewed, Carl Fulton was a 41-year-old who had done maintenance and custodial work throughout his adult life. He had done so in recent years to support his wife and two children. He is from a two-parent family in Indiana, where

71

his parents, as well as his uncles and other relatives who lived in the neighborhood, all worked in local factories. He moved to Ypsilanti as a young man to follow his brother and with the unmet wish of finding the same kind of opportunity. Ellen Martin, mother of two, was introduced in the previous chapter. Jessica Boyd is 43 and a divorced mother of three who left an abusive relationship with her former husband. In order to support her children she has worked as a domestic at her low point and a bank teller during her best times.

As Carl and Jessica said, jobs are plentiful. However, Ellen's remarks speak to precisely what kind of jobs were to be found in and near Ypsilanti throughout this time, and they generally were not believed to be good jobs. Whether black Ypsilantians were sure that work could be found or were despondent about the quality of work that was available, the simple fact of the matter is that they drew sharp distinctions in discussing the availability of jobs and the possibilities of obtaining rewarding employment. The former could be obtained with some degree of effort (and despite what Carl said, there was some considerable range in their views of how much effort it took to achieve this end). Rewarding employment, however, was far beyond the purview of most of the people in this book.

The strong belief in the availability of jobs for the people featured in this book existed because, almost to a person, they had experienced some employment in their adult lives. Those who were working certainly were not experiencing what could be called high-end employment. They could be found behind the cash register at stores or doing per diem work at construction sites on small-scale projects. Only Martin Bensen, Desmond James, Edward Jenkins, Kelly Jensen, Montel Mason, Carlton Pitts, and Sam Singleton had never experienced formal employment as adults. The work history of the others included retail food services (fast food, grocery store, or short-order cooking establishments), noncertified health-care work, general retail, office support, and custodial work.

These employment sectors capture the work histories of three-quarters of the black Ypsilantians in this book. Indeed, half of those interviewed for this project had worked in the fast-food sector at some point in their lives since turning 16. Accordingly, chronic unemployment was not the defining condition of most participants in this study. The story told here, then, is mostly about the chronically underemployed. It is about men and women who made hourly wages in the formal and informal economies. Most of them remained close to work as adults, even if they were rarely in the kind of work they most desired. As such, they were not happy with their life situations and were quite accustomed to instability and insecurity when it came to garnering work opportunity and having the capacity to make ends meet. The investment in work often meant that family social and emotional needs were rarely met with the kind of time and attention necessary for successful remediation of potential problems.

This chapter explores what going to work has meant for these individuals. In doing so, it offers another perspective on the pervasive sense of limitation that emerged as such a central part of their lives. The previous chapter addressed how place played a role in limiting their vision of opportunity. With respect to Ann Arbor, place mattered in that this city was quite proximate to them but also appeared to many of them as socially uninviting. As made more vividly apparent in this chapter, Detroit was important in that it symbolized the site for the kind of employment opportunities that made sense to them. Those opportunities, reflective of the kind of industrial order that reigned supreme in America during the middle of the twentieth century, circumscribed their evaluations of the kind of jobs they have held, what they feel about them, and what they feel is missing from them.

In looking at each of these issues, this chapter also explores the challenges that black Ypsilantians perceive as standing in the way of securing what they hold to be appropriate work for themselves. In order to achieve this goal, this chapter first explores the general sentiments about work and work opportunity of Ypsilanti's low-income African American residents. After considering what these people believe to be the state of work in their city, we explore their understandings of the challenges of finding work in a small city, and then their visions of how to manage the struggle of work-family obligations.

The contrast between black Ypsilantians' visions of what exists for them and what they would like to exist elucidates much about how they make sense of their local prospects. More tellingly, however, men and women differed in how they explained what they believe exists for them. These differences have much to do with who has access to or experience in lower-tier work in sectors that seem to translate into possible careers (the women) and those who have access to what seems to be dead-end work (the men).

THE QUALITY OF WORK IN YPSILANTI

The first chapter told how important factory work was for the mid- to late-twentieth-century identity of Ypsilanti and its African American residents. It should not come as a surprise, then, that most conversations about work, especially about notions of good work and desirable work, pivoted in some way or another around a focus on the factory. The decline of the factory as a prominent place of employment was the standard narrative about the decline of good work prospects in the city. Even for the women, who either did not imagine ever doing such work or did not feel that one day they would want to do it, their understanding was that the factory was central to stabilizing secure work and visions of future opportunity in Ypsilanti.

Lori Watson is a 20-year-old mother who left her job as a parking garage clerical worker during her pregnancy. As she put it:

> There's less and less plants now . . . so, uh, it might be a little harder [to find good work]. Um, but then people are still working in the plants. I know my uncle's been working in the plant for like 20 years. And I know people who have been working in there for longer than that. . . . Those are good paying jobs then. You didn't really need an education at that time. But now, um, I think you can still find a decent job. I mean, it won't be the best, but you can still find a job.

At the time of his interview, 21-year-old Montel Mason had never worked as an adult, even though he had graduated from high school and enrolled in some community college courses. He explained:

> I don't feel that secure. Sometimes I can't sleep at night, tossing and turning 'cause I don't know tomorrow what's going to happen. It's like it's closing in on me and I do have family that I can go to, but I mean I'm all I got really, you know. . . . I don't feel that secure without a degree. Now, once I get a degree, then I could feel a little bit more secure, but from my understanding, I was once told that just because you got a degree don't mean you're going to get a job.

These sentiments make sense in the context of the demise of high-quality work opportunity in Ypsilanti. Recall that these people reside in a small town that established itself by the proliferation of factory work. Throughout the mid- to late twentieth century, African American Ypsilanti residents found their way into automobile plants or the various industries that emerged and were sustained by the existence of such plants (e.g., food and customer services, small retail businesses). If there was a member of the family working in a plant or at a local hospital, then unionized benefits such as health care, insurance, and membership in a credit union (which provided professional financial services and assistance) were a part of that family's or household's situation. However, factory jobs were now virtually gone, and much of what was done in the factory on the assembly line was done by machines. Hence, the proliferation of technology in the workplace meant that a consistent threat to work stability and security was an ever-present concern for many blue-collar workers in Ypsilanti. Whether employed or not, many black Ypsilantians wavered between talking about the good jobs of the past or the anxiety of the present in their discussions of experiencing work.

The absence of meaningful career-building work for black Ypsilantians was the result of Ypsilanti's having benefited from the automobile manufacturing industry that was headquartered in greater southeastern Michigan. Almost all of the residents pointed to some period in the past when nearly everyone seemed to have had not just a job, but a career in that sector. The physical plant of the city is a testament to that past. A three-minute drive going east on Harriet Street, which cuts through the census tracts where most of these residents live, puts one just north of a former Ford Motor Company plant, resting on 45 acres of land and containing one million square feet of space. It was the site of close to 3,000 jobs in its heyday in the mid-twentieth century. That plant, which spun off from Ford to become a Visteon plant, produced car starters, ignition coils, distributors, horns, struts, air conditioning clutches, and bumper shock devices. It had maintained a gradually shrinking workforce in recent decades, housing about 1,800 jobs in 1982 and about 500 in 2005. It closed in 2008.

Along the part of Michigan Avenue that runs through the center of Ypsilanti, one encounters a series of neighborhood diners, fast-food restaurants, and small shops where inexpensive meals, cell phones and calling plans, hardware, and other easily consumable items are for sale. These stores contain the very kinds of jobs that African Americans in Ypsilanti claimed existed for people like themselves. The jobs offer little in terms of secure wages and long-term employment. Hence, black Ypsilantians readily admit that jobs are available in their city. What they do not say, and what they do not believe, is that these jobs provide the kinds

of meaningful income or social status that people desire from employment.

Upon being asked about the kinds of jobs most readily available for
men like himself, Jerry Jackson, who has been unemployed for most of
his adult life, flatly said, "McDonald's, Burger King."

Similarly, Sam Singleton, a 21-year-old who has been chronically unemployed and lives with his girlfriend, said:

> Ain't nothing out there for nobody. It ain't nothing out there. I mean,
> the only thing out there is fast food . . . If you did just go for your GED,
> I mean, that acquires you a job, but, you know what I'm saying, it don't
> mean you can have a top-notch job. I mean, that could just qualify you
> to be the hiring manager at McDonald's and you getting paid $9 an
> hour and everyone else getting paid $6, $7, $8, you know.[1]

The rise of lower-tier employment opportunities that began in the mid-
1990s was not lost on black Ypsilantians. When asked about the kinds of
jobs that exist for people like themselves, each of them identified this
trend by stating that certain kinds of jobs were readily available.

Brock Bevins is a 37-seven-year old who has served time in a state
penitentiary. His only work experience is as a temporary employee stock-
ing shelves in retail establishments. As he stated upon being asked about
the kinds of jobs a person could find right now if he or she was looking
for work, "The little factory jobs, cleaning, little menial jobs . . . that just
enough to get by on."

Twenty-eight-year-old Carter Gaston once earned as much at $15.00
an hour as an office clerk. He also worked for $18.00 an hour in a small
factory as a package deliverer. He said:

> The factory, period. That's it. You know what I'm saying? Construc-
> tion, a bad job. As soon as they through, you don't got no job no more.
> Bad job like that is available for people with my level of intelligence,
> working skills. But, primarily the factory, though. And, then, it's a
> three-year waiting period to get in there, you know, but, uh, you have
> to wait. It's a waiting process.

When asked about the types of jobs that she believes exist today for
blacks with a similar level of education and work experience as herself,
Elena Perry, age 22, said, "Fast food, retail, factories, well you can get in
the hospital, but it's like, in the cafeteria in the hospital, or transferring
patients, stuff like that. . . . Because that's all I've been given and I want
more. I don't really want fast food and stuff like that."

Kelly Jensen dropped out of high school before graduating. At age 18, her brief exposure to work included janitorial service and temporary office work. She said, "Fast food, clothing stores, working at the hospital. It just depends on you and what you want. But, it's getting to now where if you don't even have a high school diploma, you can't even get a job at McDonald's."

While black Ypsilantians explained that work could be found, the problem remained trying to find work that provided the kind of security and monetary return that would allow them to support their families. The kinds of jobs that they believed to be available were situated in per diem or short-term arrangements, or if long term and more stable, provided no fringe benefits or promotion opportunities. Consequently, each of them made clear that the problem was not the absence of work, but the absence of employment opportunities that allowed one to function as an effective provider for oneself and one's family.

Twenty-year-old Sharon Jett briefly attended community college. She also worked as a cashier in a fast-food restaurant. Her extra schooling provided her with a slightly greater sense of accomplishment than those in her social circle. This was evident in her explanation of the world of work:

> Well, I'm a fairly educated person, I'd say more educated than a lot of people my age, because most people my age either never got into college, or didn't graduate high school, and I've done both, you know, graduated high school and at least started college. You know, I have to go back and finish. I have a lot of work experience. I've got a lot of my own personal skill set. As far as someone on my level, I'd say there are a lot of jobs available for someone on my level . . . office jobs. Jobs where an interpreter is required. I'd say jobs in the computer industry. I'd say jobs where vocal is very important, like phone jobs, jobs where you use the phone a lot. Um, I can't really think of anything else.

As much as black Ypsilantians believed that work could be found in their city, they also admitted to feeling insecure about such work prospects. The belief that one could find work was not matched by the belief that such work was stable. For instance, although Carl Fulton said that jobs are available in Ypsilanti, he also said the following about whether job security is a reality:

> Not at all. Not at all. I could walk in and feel like any minute I'm gonna be terminated. At every job that I've had. At every one of them. I think

uh, people try to make you feel inferior and also a lot of white guys will make you feel like, you know, we can get rid of you any time we want. They won't say it, but . . . if their buddy come up in there, you gone. You know, I don't care what kind of credentials you got, Mr. Black Man, you can be gone. We can make something up to make sure you leave, or just piss you off to where you say, "Look I got to go."

Karen Andrews was particularly assertive in making her case about job security in the world of work. She said:

There is no such thing as job security. You understand what I'm saying? No such thing because you can always be replaced with somebody better, somebody younger, somebody older, somebody smarter. You can always be replaced. And then with technology in, we may all as far as humans be replaced. . . . We could never have a total, you know, robotic world, but . . . it could cause a major crisis if companies you know, started to use more modern technology, started to do these robot things there could be a crisis for lots of people.

After pausing to collect her thoughts, she went on to say:

Depending on your experience and your skills, it's pretty hard now because a lot of it is based on, they want a lot of education background . . . I don't know. . . . I guess, it's some employers just being greedy, looking out for themselves. . . . Some actually think that the job is not worth as much. . . . And some employers know that there's people out there with not many skills . . . that will settle for that, because nobody else would hire them. So it's always going to be people out there who didn't graduate from college, who didn't graduate from high school, who don't know how to read real good, who don't know how to write real good. That they're going to eat. They that can get for $5.50, and some people that settle for that, cause they feel like that's all they can do. And they intend to do better. They said they'd do better, but usually it never happens.

As is the case in many cities in America, large or small, Ypsilanti was defined by the kind of work that many of the residents did, and the public image of those residents was defined by their jobs. That is because work is both what one does and who one is. It gives identity to both people and places and is central to creating a sense of order and structure in personal and community life (Sweet and Meiksins 2013; Hodson 2001; Muirhead 2007; Budd 2011; Gini 2001). As social psychologist Erik H. Erikson said, "Nothing else in our lives can give us the sense of objective identity that work can" (quoted in Gini 2001, 5). The strong identity of the worker throughout the twentieth century in Ypsilanti was tied to the automobile plant. Not only was this kind of work crafted into the public identity of people in this city, but going to work in this capacity meant that much of everyday life was organized, routinized, and structured by plant work (Gini 2001).

For black Ypsilantians, a life that was not anchored in consistent and meaningful work meant suffering a nebulous if not altogether negative identity. A part of the struggle regarding work, then, was that while it existed, the kind that did was not highly valued. Most important, it certainly was not the kind that had existed in previous decades in Ypsilanti, which had brought about a sense of positive identity. Therefore, the kind of work that many people in this book did, and the city in which they did it, situated them to look back to a past when better work existed, but that work was no longer plentiful. Indeed, high-quality factory jobs were virtually gone, and much of what was done in the factory on the assembly line struck black Ypsilantians as now being done by machines. The proliferation of technology in the workplace meant that a consistent threat to work stability and security was an ever-present concern for many who saw the machine as something that could replace them or minimize their centrality to the job.

TECHNOLOGY IN YPSILANTI'S WORLD OF WORK

Even if it was not fully comprehensible to them, black Ypsilantians were aware of the increased importance of technology in the workplace. When discussing the modern world of work, they often referred to technology when identifying what differentiated the past world of work from the present. In talking about work in the modern era, Brock Bevins said, "Like now they got everything high tech, and it's so much like even the little jobs that people used to do, robots do 'em."

Brock did not provide any detailed examples of what robots were doing and how they might be changing the world of work. The common discussion of technology by black Ypsilantians included references to its prevalence and how it minimized contemporary work opportunities for them. Their comments did not include precise arguments about how they had managed the proliferation of technology or of how they might do so. In fact, almost half of the black Ypsilantians featured here argued that a current condition of work was the increased presence of technology.

They understood this condition as resulting in the reduction of workers in the very sectors that used to provide what they understood to be "good" jobs, but the depth of their understanding rarely went beyond that level of awareness.

Thirty-seven-year-old Tonisha Rawls is a high school graduate who did commercial cleaning as well as some clerical work when she was employed. Her take on the issue follows:

> Well, bein' that we are really in a technical age, a lot of jobs are not there anymore. A lot of people are, aptin' to work for theyselves like I am. They're takin' what they know, and have learned in college, and doin' it right then, or they're pullin' out of the corporations sometime.

The changing nature of work opportunity in Ypsilanti was not lost on black Ypsilantians. Although they could not say much about exactly how technology was changing the nature of work in their city, they did attest that it had done so. The few who did offer precise comments about how technology was affecting the current world of work had work experiences in Ann Arbor (especially at the University of Michigan), even if their actual jobs were not technological in any substantive way.

For example, Vance Ritchie is a 23-three-year-old who graduated from high school but was fired from his job as a custodian at the University of Michigan after he was arrested for workplace infractions. He was one of five black Ypsilantians in this book who reported working in Ann Arbor for a sustained amount of time. The exposure to that city afforded him a distinct perspective on the role of technology in shaping the contemporary world of work. However, that vantage point did not result in a clear and coherent message about how one could properly navigate a technologically saturated world of work. In trying to explain the modern world of work, which for him included work opportunities in Ypsilanti and Ann Arbor, Vance said:

> I mean, there is so many jobs, so many different things to do. I mean, landscaping, groundwork, janitorial, fast food, clerical, technical jobs— technical, computer or work with computers, working on computers, like wiring, technical, the electrical part of when people build houses. Working on cars. Let me see. . . . Yeah, there are . . . there are so many that, I mean, that . . . our black people are doing. I mean, how they got the job is basically wanting the job, wanting to apply for the job. A lot of them have an interest and maybe some experience, you know. It's not all about education, but education helps out so much. I mean, they

say, okay, you went to the place and you studied about this job, I mean, you know, this is what you're going to do, and we have an opening you most likely will get it.

In trying to properly place himself in this amalgamation of current opportunities, he said:

I don't think I have enough education. I feel insecure. So I would say I'm still dealing with the jobs I might not like or they don't pay as much as I wish it would, but I'm still young and I'm still not done with college, so I kind of have to respect that, I kind of have to accept it.

For black Ypsilantians, insecurity in regard to employment was due not only to what they perceived to be an absence of good work, but also to the increased presence of technology in the workplace. Unlike those with more education and more familiarity, technology was not perceived to facilitate new opportunities but rather to foreclose upon the kinds of opportunities that made sense to black Ypsilantians. Rather than being curious about new opportunities, they were anxious about the erasure of older, more familiar ones.

WORK OPPORTUNITIES AND FAMILY CHALLENGES IN THE SPACE OF A SMALL CITY

Ypsilanti did not simply lack the kind of jobs that would allow its African Americans residents to feel more secure about the world of work. It also lacked the kind of physical infrastructure—a vibrant downtown business community—that would allow them to envision where good jobs might be. In order for those less familiar with small cities to understand this, consider how easy it is for residents of large cities to think of work opportunities that include white-collar office work of various types, coupled with an expansive retail sector composed of department stores and specialty shops. Ypsilanti was too small a city to contain any of this. Consequently, its residents could not point to a vibrant and bustling downtown region as a site for good jobs. The type of good job found in large cities — in skyscraper office buildings or financial districts—is not visible to residents of small cities, at least not in the same way that lower-income people who live in large cities might envision.

In the latter case, a downtown district often serves as a physical anchor for how residents think about work. The relationship of physical space to good jobs operates differently in small cities. Lower-income residents of such cities often refer to good jobs as being someplace else rather than talking about where they can be found in their own city. Furthermore, in an era when manufacturing reigned supreme, the factory, wherever it was located (and never much in the downtown region of small cities) was where good jobs were to be found. Hence, when it comes to talking about good jobs, the problem for low-income people living in a small city is not simply restricted to the paucity of good employment prospects relative to what may be available in larger cities. Instead, it is also a matter of that which is unseen or invisible to people who have only the small city context in which to make sense of work and work opportunity. The good job, then, is both physically and imaginatively distant. Consequently, it gets articulated without an accompanying vivid sense of precisely where or how it may be found.

That being said, in a city on the doorstep of the automobile manufacturing center of America, meaningful work for black Ypsilantians never strayed far from focusing in some way on the automobile plant. For some, the plant was the model of optimal work. An example comes from 28-year-old Dante Ellis. His work history involves serving as a short-order cook and as a laborer in an auto body shop. He said, "Right now a lot of blacks go to Ford. A lot of blacks are Ford, G.M., factory jobs, construction jobs, city jobs, like that."

Dante's best evidence for this is that his brother-in-law works at a Ford plant. The African Americans that Dante knows about in the automobile plant work alongside his brother-in-law. While Dante reported that such jobs brought forth material benefits, he also argued that they brought forth difficulties as well:

> I talk about getting in the factory a lot, but you know, right now that's for a lot of the black people and, you know, that's good money. But my brother-in-law he gets up at 3 o'clock in the morning. He gets up at 3 o'clock in the morning. You know he makes lots of money, you know, makes good money. He's always too tired to do anything and, you know.

Another way in which the plant was imbedded in how black Ypsilantians thought about work was conveyed by Sabel Janis. She was 31 years old when interviewed. Sabel was unemployed at that time but had worked as a clerical in a temporary capacity. She had three children and lived with her boyfriend, and she had attended community college for a short while.

Her mother and stepfather, as well as several extended family members, all worked in Ford Motor Company plants. When talking about her father, she said, "He liked the plant because it's good money. . . . You get so many years in there it's real, you know, good money."

The actual assembly line work was not what she found appealing. As she explained when discussing her parents' jobs:

> They just said they worked in a plant. I never knew what the inside of the plant looked like. I just knew that they made cars. Um, I wasn't aware of their wages or anything like that. I just know that they used to come home tired. Like my mother, she had blood clots in her legs and stuff and they had to get her a sitting job and I was like eight or nine and I kept witnessing her in and out of the hospital, off from work. My father's back, I seen his back just go out on him while he was walking and stuff. So they really embedded in my head that the factory is not where I wanted to be when I got older.

However, one uncle who was college educated had a desk job at one of the plants. In discussing him she said, "He was in the office part because he went to college. That's my father's brother. He's the one that got my father in there, so I know he was satisfied."

Despite the work-related challenges affecting her parents, Sabel testified that her family found the factory work rewarding even if she felt that this was not the kind of opportunity she wanted:

> My aunts, I believe they were satisfied because they were single also and that's the way they supported their family. And the plant is like the better paying jobs to support and put food on the table. I never heard any complaints from them and they're still there. You know, it's been like 30 years. I think they're pretty satisfied.

The vision of black Ypsilantians resembles that of residents of single-industry cities (Dudley 1994; Milkman 1997). This is because everything that they might imagine or hope to do in terms of good work was an extension of their vision of what people like them used to do in prior years, which delivered financial and status-based rewards. Operating without any proximate sense of a white-collar business district, a fashion district, a dot-com sector, or any other urban community that reflected material success, the talk of accessible good jobs rested solely in the imagination of what used to be good work in Ypsilanti.

My realization of the significance of the physical design of the small city in how black Ypsilantians thought about work was a gradual process. I surely knew that space mattered in how people thought about opportunity. A major part of my research career prior to going to Ypsilanti involved studying how economically challenged Chicago-based African American men talked about the kinds of jobs available in the downtown areas of the cities in which they lived (Young 2000, 2004). Those men sometimes offered highly imaginative accounts of what kinds of job existed in the downtown area because they actually spent very little time in contact with those areas, the people who worked in them, or the kinds of job opportunities available to them. That being the case, some of the men whom I studied would reference the "suits and ties" of the people who worked in downtown Chicago or the desk jobs located in the immense office buildings in that part of the city. Consequently, even if they knew little about the actual content of the good life and the work experiences of those with good jobs, an easily identifiable and locatable place was a consistent point of reference for them.

For black Ypsilantians, often no such easily identifiable spatial references surfaced. Instead, their city housed plenty of what they regarded as bad and less than decent jobs. Good jobs simply were referred to as existing elsewhere. Very few argued that such jobs were in Ann Arbor. As we have seen previously, they could only place these jobs as existing somewhere other than in Ypsilanti. While references to good jobs could not be geographically grounded (i.e., located in a specific business district or a downtown area, save for the very few black Ypsilantians who referred to Ann Arbor), such jobs were often situated as being in a factory or plant. References to good work, then, meant having to think beyond their city in an effort to locate where such work might be, or such work was understood to be a remnant of family or community history (i.e., the plants throughout southeastern Michigan or elsewhere that older relatives worked in, or the plants that used to be functional in Ypsilanti). A virtue of the large city is that good jobs could be identified, or at least imagined, in a spatial context. Often that context was downtown. The spatial context circumscribing the lives of black Ypsilantians demanded a very different kind of thinking about good jobs.

A major consequence of the very different kind of thinking that went on among black Ypsilantians was a consistent reference to the challenge of transportation in finding, as well as getting to and from, work. Transportation was the most commonly referred to obstacle to securing jobs (raised by over two-thirds of the black Ypsilantians). For example, Brock

Bevins said, "It's not hard to find a job, but to find one that's gonna support you, you have to, you need transportation. . . . And most of the jobs that they got, are not on a bus line so people can get to 'em. They got them a way out there. So you need reliable transportation also."

Larry Lawson, a 35-year-old whose only work experience was as a parking garage attendant, put it succinctly when he said, "Transportation and location, getting there, you know what I'm saying?"

The participants' preoccupation with transportation was such that nothing else mattered if one had no means of actually getting to work. Transportation was an important point of emphasis, because it was so hard for black Ypsilantians to envision precisely where good jobs could be found in their city. Yet, without knowing exactly where the good jobs were, value was often placed on the idea of transportation as much as on precisely where that transportation could take them.

In supporting that assertion, Jerry Jackson said, "What I don't have is transportation. That's the number one problem 'cause I don't have any transportation whatsoever to get a job. So in order to get a good job that's the first question they ask you, 'Do you have transportation,' when you're looking for a good job. You say no, then you don't get the job."

Martin Bensen was a 24-year-old with a GED who was working as a truck loader for $8.50 an hour when he was interviewed. He had been in and out of employment throughout his adult life and was still living at home with his mother. He also had been incarcerated. He was the father of one child. As he explained, "I go to other places but, in our area they're not really hiring. . . . They're in Belleville, or like in Pleasantville, or in Tecumseh [small Michigan cities, each located between 15 and 45 minutes from Ypsilanti] , somewhere like that you know."

In the previous decades the presence of a large factory in Ypsilanti had created the appearance of opportunity. The factory, then, served in Ypsilanti as would a downtown district in a large city (or, as is the case of Ann Arbor, a research-intensive higher educational institution in a college town).[2] However, without large-scale factories or a bustling downtown district being visible to black Ypsilantians, it was much harder for them to precisely ascertain the physical location of today's good jobs. What they could ascertain is that they needed a means to get away from Ypsilanti to find the kind of work that made sense to them. This is why a lack of transportation was so consistently defined as a problem in their experiences with work.

Aside from external barriers such as transportation, the major obstacles that black Ypsilantians reported to finding a good job were lack of education and lack of experience with good jobs. This is not surprising, as it is consistent with what many low-income African Americans report as the personal deficits they have when it comes to employment readiness (Hochschild 1995; Mincy 2006; Young 2004). However, other deficits remained. Most of these had to do with the absence of benefits in the kinds of jobs available to many of them.

Carl Fulton said the following while discussing the importance of health-care benefits: "That is like the number one thing. Oh, man, because I got a doctor bill for $3,500 for one day. Oh, God! And my Blue Cross Blue Shield didn't cover it. Health insurance I think is the number one issue in my life."

Carl, who was speaking prior to the creation of the Affordable Care Act (which provided Americans with wider access to health care), elaborated upon this point by talking about how employers prevent workers from being able to get health coverage:

> You got jobs now days will not give you any health coverage for 90 days. You could die in 90 days. And then most of the places are only going to let you work up to 89 days so they don't have to cover you on the health care, and then re-hire you. Or either they're gonna be temporary services where they don't have to pay hardly no health insurance on you if you do get hurt. You should be covered from day one when you get your job. No matter what the government, our own government should say you're gonna be covered from day one. What if you trip and fall and hurt your leg and you have no health insurance because they say, "Well you didn't work here for 90 days." What are you gonna do? You gonna have to go to the ADC [Aid to Families with Dependent Children, or AFDC] system and then they're gonna say, well you should a came here before this happened to you. So health coverage is a big issue and it's gone to the point to where it's gone to the extent to silly.

Ellen Martin said that a job that pays well is more crucial than a job that one might enjoy, and that it needs to come with benefits and flexibility. As she put it:

> Because income is more important than what you enjoy. You're not going to enjoy everything you do because you're not working for yourself, so how can you enjoy that? . . . Um, if I found a job that paid at least $10.50 an hour, or at least $10 at the most, and you get paid every

week with benefits. I would be happy, you know, with that. . . . I just like the straight hours shift. I don't like the swing shift. That's what I just got off of. I don't like that, because [of] the kids. If I didn't have the kids, it wouldn't matter. . . . It needs to be nearby. At least, I would say, 20 minutes [away] at the most.

Karen Andrews shared this sentiment:

> I'd rather take less money with good benefits than a job with, you know, a lot more money but shitty benefits. 'Cause that's what you need, that health insurance, that you know, life insurance, whatever. You need those things, you know, and that's more important when you got uh, you know, a $10,000 hospital bill and your insurance only paying, well I don't know, 50% or whatever. Five thousand dollars is a lot of money to come up with. So I think when you've got a good plan, a good insurance plan . . . [the job is] much better. . . .The location is important cause I want to be able, you know, to get there, you know, on time, and get home to my kids quickly. And of course if something happens, I wouldn't be able to get there within an ample amount of time. So I ain't goin' to take nothing down in Detroit, not right now. . . . I ain't about to you know, take a job down there, and somethin' happen and I got to get back here. . . . I ain't about to do that. . . . If you got kids you spend two hours getting to work and most of the time you sleep. You can't be a proper parent.

Thirty-nine-year-old Aletha Mack is a high school graduate who worked as a nurse's aide when she was employed. Speaking along the same lines as the others, she said:

> I lost a job because my daughter had pneumonia and I'm at the hospital with her. I didn't know she had pneumonia, but she kept running a temp and I took her to the emergency room. And, I called my job and let them know I was going to be late, and I'm like, "Yeah, I'm going to be a little late. I'm at the emergency room with my daughter, and, uh, as soon as I leave here, depending on what kind of instructions they give me, I'll be back to work." So, the doctor saw her and everything and ran a test and told me she had pneumonia. She had pneumonia that I didn't know she had. All this meant that she had to stay in the hospital for at least seven days and take all this medication and I didn't have nobody to keep her, because me and her dad had broke up. He was here, but we had broke up. And, I didn't have a choice but to let them know that I would need a couple of days off work. And, they told me No. I'm like, "Well, I need to take some personal days off," and I'm not—I never take no personal days off. "Well, you can't take no person-

al days." I'm like, "Why not?" "We need you now, we're short staffed and this and that." I said, "Well, you know what? My daughter comes first, because [I] only got one daughter and if she dies today, y'all wouldn't care. So, if y'all choose to fire me because I want to stay at home a couple of days and take care of my daughter, then fire me." And, they did.

If good work was not available, family-based problems and crises certainly were. For each of the participants, then, this meant that some kind of work had to be avoided because the returns on investing in it did not help circumvent or minimize family problems. Accordingly, the solution for the work-family divide for the black Ypsilantians that experienced it was not simply putting work first, but considering whether and how the available work options could be made to mesh with the kind of family situation that one was experiencing. Depending on the quality of that situation, some kinds of work—that which involved extensive travel away from home, that which paid wages so low that travel to work and other work-related expenses severely reduced one's income, or that which was short term and thus prevented effective long-term planning for family security—had to be avoided all together.

For those black Ypsilantians who experienced consistent employment, another dimension of challenge was the management of family and work demands. Presumably, work should deliver monetary and other benefits for oneself and one's family. The context of lower-tier work, however, is such that effectively maintaining it can involve risking one's availability to be of service to one's family.

Black Ypsilantians were caught in a world of deprivation. The kinds of jobs that they regarded as essential for achieving family stability and security—the kinds with fringe benefits and union membership—had been quite plentiful in a bygone era in Ypsilanti. The kinds of jobs that they believed were now easily accessible provided minimal material rewards, little job security, and no fringe benefit support. We turn now to a few stories about the struggle with meeting family obligations in a world of less-than-fulfilling work.

Recall from chapter 2 that Brian Fuller was in a most precarious situation. His daughters were removed from his home, and his recent release from jail meant he had an extraordinarily brief postrelease work history. His fiancée, the mother of his children, was nearing completion of her studies to become a nurse's assistant, and he was working for a landscaping company until he could land a permanent job.

In chapter 2 we saw how Brian approached balancing the effort concerning work with his interest in being a consistently visible father at home. He explained that he chose to spend more time at work so that more income could be generated. For now, work would always have to get the attention.

Carl Fulton did not face the same kinds of pressures that confronted Brian. Carl had no criminal record, and his children lived at home with him and his partner. What Carl was lacking, however, was the time to commit to being a part of his children's lives in the way that he hoped he could. He said that he accepted whatever extra work opportunities became available at his job because he wanted to someday reproduce the kind of family life for his children that he had experienced as a child, which meant having meals at home with his siblings and parents and enjoying quality time with his parents despite the fact that they had 11 other children for whom to care. As he explained:

> I have to work more and more and harder and it's not enough time in the day for me. . . . I've gotten super hyper and it got to a point to where I was . . . not [having] a nervous breakdown, but there's not enough time for me to do anything. It's not enough time for me to even think.

As far as how his children served as a motivating factor for him, Carl went on to say:

> I wanted more stuff for them. Everything for them. . . . And I'd say, "Man I gotta get more money and get more stuff." I want them to be happy. I want happy, happy. "I want you all to be happy. I want you to have things that I never had. I want you to have everything that I always wanted." I can't do it. I have to change my thinking. But right now if I could just make enough money to get these apartments [to one day buy some property]. Ooh. I want to stay home.

For Carl, staying home did not mean never going back to work. Instead, he wanted the chance to control his capacity to be at home regularly with his children, a situation that he was far from experiencing in his life. Like Brian, Carl clearly saw his role in the family as the core material provider (although, like Brian, he fully supported his partner's right, and actually necessity, to go to work). Hence, he went to work on as many assignments as he could get in addition to his regular duties. However, the desire to be at home was a salient part of his quest for a better life as well.

Ellen Martin also preferred to narrow the distance between work and home. However, as her husband was recovering from his near-life-ending situation, her interest in doing so was for reasons that drastically differed from Carl's and Brian's. Although Ellen's husband was well into his recovery from the shooting, she explained that he still had limited capacity to function in the household. This meant that Ellen had to serve as the primary material provider as well as the caretaker of the home, even though she was part of a two-parent household. When explaining the unique way in which she was faced with having to manage the work-family divide, Ellen said:

> Because sometimes if he's not well or something like that, he cannot watch them [the children], and then I barely have a babysitter because I moved out here, and I have no family out here but him. So, that's the hard thing. It's really hard having a baby. Right now, that's what I'm going through. I had to quit my job because I didn't have nobody to watch them for four hours, and this was a good job.

Although the reasons differ, the stress that Ellen felt was shared by Karen, who was insistent that good work for parents who care about their children had to include provisions for being able to respond to family emergencies whenever necessary. As she said:

> I mean, when they sick, they sick. You gotta stay home. Sometimes you can't help it. . . . Even when you want to go to work, if they sick you just can't go. . . . You have to worry about, you know, who's gonna baby sit. Who's gonna pay the baby sitter? Where can you get a baby sitter for cheap? So you have to go through all that, so child care's a major issue. . . . It would be much easier to say, O.K., I can work this shift or that shift because then you have to limit what you do, you have to limit what shift you can work because you got, you know, a family.

Unlike more privileged people, who can afford to turn to professional support mechanisms in times of crisis or unexpected emergencies, people like Karen, Brian, and Carl have nothing more than themselves and their partners to turn to for help, and Ellen barely had that option available to her. As illustrated by each of them, the problem is exacerbated by the fact that the kinds of work opportunities available to them are often those least likely to provide flexibility when family crises emerge. In fact, Karen has had extensive personal experience with jobs that do not allow much leeway for handling family crises. As a case example, she explained what had happened at one prior job:

> It was just to the point where this job was um, they give you like eight occurrences a year (to be late or absent, irrespective of the reasons why). . . . If you're late one minute, it don't matter. Or, if you totally missed a day or whatever. So you got eight per year and even if say your child got sick. I worked midnights. If your child got sick at 4 o'clock in the afternoon and you was in emergency room till 11:30 and you brought in this note, it don't matter. It still counts against you for the simple fact you was not there. And so, you know, it comes to a point in time where you gotta say, okay, it's either this job or my kids.

In discussing how she has handled the constraints that have emerged in trying to keep a job while dealing with family emergencies, she said:

> I've had jobs where my kids was up at work with me. . . . I didn't have a baby sitter . . . and some of 'em who don't have kids don't understand. Some with kids do, but a lot without don't. . . . And so it makes it kind of harder to deal with them since they don't really know.

As people who are situated as being no higher than lower-tier working class, black Ypsilantians are most familiar with jobs that pay by the hour and contain little, if any, flexibility if problems outside of work emerge. This means that rather than simply experiencing a sense of consternation or disappointment about being unable to commit to their families as much as they would like to, such people must quite literally risk losing their jobs in order to deal with family pressures.

Men like Carl and Brian have explained that, at least thus far in their lives, they have committed to going to work in order to provide for their families rather than to spending more time with their families. However, both men have the luxury of having partners or spouses who are able to respond to family pressures first. In contrast, women like Ellen Martin cannot effectively rely on their partners to handle the family needs (at least not at present), and Karen Andrews has decided to commit to what she believes is crucial time with her children rather than to finding a better job, which she thought would require her to have less involvement in her children's everyday lives.

In the fourth chapter much more is said about good jobs. That chapter discusses much more about how black Ypsilantians make sense of that concept, especially what it means as a reference to what they imagine instead of what they have actually experienced as workers. For now, we turn to matters of race, which is another critical dimension of how black Ypsilantians have experienced work.

EXPERIENCING RACE IN THE WORLD OF WORK

A central part of the black American experience involves thinking about the effects of race on one's life (Feagin and Sikes 1994; St. Jean and Feagan 1997; Hochschild 1995; Pew Research Center 2016; Young 2004). However, it may not always be evident how differently that thinking unfolds across different geographic regions and contexts. For black Ypsilantians, thinking about race is not based on a life rooted in extreme racial residential segregation. Ypsilanti is not racially segregated in the ways that larger cities in America have been. Social relationships, at least for the black Ypsilantians in this book, often do take the form of same-race associations.[3] However, given the smallness of Ypsilanti and its proximity to predominantly white residential communities, it is not uncommon to see white Americans in neighborhoods that are within a 15-minute walk from the places where the people in this book live. Consequently, race is not a defining feature of geographic isolation for black Ypsilantians. As we have already seen, race surfaces in black Ypsilantians' thoughts about place mostly by their referencing of neighboring Ann Arbor as a more traditional "white" space in comparison to their own city. Yet even though Ypsilanti is more comfortable to them, it is not necessarily a place that lacks the presence of white Americans. Hence, while the majority of black Ypsilantians do see race as a factor in everyday life, they do so in ways that are distinct to the small city experience. The proximity of white Americans means that any retreat into blackness occurs only if one remains within the space of his or her household or residential block.

Only four black Ypsilantians in this study explicitly reported that race was not an issue in their work experiences. They did not declare that race did not matter as a larger societal issue, but only in regard to their work experiences. For example, Geri Benton, a 28-year-old who had attended community college and worked only in the fast-food industry, explained, "I personally have never had a problem being black and not, you know, being passed up for a job or something like that. But, I think that if I came in here chewing gum and flashy, all that, I think that would have an effect on, you know, if they want to hire me or not."

Another of these four, Justine Wells, is 24. She also attended community college. She was a clerical worker for the University of Michigan for several years, but otherwise was unemployed save for a short period as an assembly line worker. She said, "Some people won't feel secure about [work] because they always think a job is picking a certain person over them, or a white person over them. It's not always that way. It depends how you come into the workplace filling out the application and how you act when you're in there, how you ask for the application."

A third participant, Dante Ellis, is a 28-year-old short-order cook who also paints cars. He said, "I'm working for ten years. I've only had three jobs in my whole life. . . . Never like any racism or anything."

Explicit acknowledgment of the role of racism in work experience, even if only briefly, was made by all other participants. While they did not always claim that racism alone kept them out of work, they did believe that it limited their employment chances. As Carl Fulton said, "Even some fast food restaurants won't hire you. Um, because you're black. They don't want to have to deal with you."

For all others, race was central to their work experience. In a story that conveys the common feeling that race was a central part of how employers treated black Ypsilantians, Kelly Jensen, who had never held a job in her young life but reported having looked for work after she became a mother, said the following:

> Some people look at you for your color and they won't hire you because of that. It just depends on where you go. . . . It's rude how they talk to you. . . . They don't talk to other people like that. Like, a person that's white could sit right there, and they don't say that to them, but they could say that to you. And, that hurts my feelings. I don't like being disgraced because of my color. That's one thing I hate the most.

Along the same lines, Carter Gaston, a high school graduate who was a clerical worker during the few years that he was employed as an adult, said:

> Sit-down jobs where you're working with white people, corporate jobs and stuff like that, man, it's a different ballgame. . . . The difference between working with white people is that they just have no intention of you stepping on they platform, period. At least working with your own people, you got a chance, you know what I'm saying. . . . But, with white folk . . . it's just not going to happen, you know what I'm saying?

In making his argument, Gaston compared his experiences in clerical services with his time spent in prison. He explained that incarceration was his first serious encounter with the power of racism:

> I appreciate my prison experience, because that was definitely a wake-up call in many, many ways. Then you know what to expect, which is the finer thing about prison. You know what to expect every day. One thing don't change. When you wake up and that gate break, it's some racist white people on the other side, for sure. You know, they ain't going to change, period. They ain't going to change. Even if they had a good day at home last night, they ain't going to change. You know what to expect.

Returning to his experiences at work, he said, "Out here [outside of prison], it's a little different. They close the door, they lights stay on, they sit at a round table, and they talk about ruining your black life in private. Ain't that a bitch?"

For the few black Ypsilantians who had had such experiences, access to white-collar work environments helped fortify understandings of blackness as a liability in the world of work. It was in these environments that black Ypsilantians felt themselves to be hyper-subordinate, especially as they held lower-tier positions when working in such places.

Aletha Mack said:

> [White Americans] just treat black people—I don't know, maybe they still got that slave thing, but they treat white people with more respect. I still think if somebody is going in, like, you know, you go to fill out the application for the same thing, you know, I think the white person will get it.

Ted Cummings is a 20-year-old who took some community college courses and worked as a short-order cook. He said:

> I don't hate white folks, but I want to do better than the white folks. I want to do better than the white folks where I work at, only because— and, I'm not saying it's a really good thing, but the way I was raised [by his mother], it's like everything you do, you got to show them. . . . They might not have a lot of contact with black folks, so you got to show them you can do—you can show them that you're as good as them or better than them.

Thirty-seven-year-old Mark Niles attended community college for a short while and then worked as a custodian for Ypsilanti public housing. He told the following story about working on a remodeling project:

They had me on that roof, carrying . . . not doing any carpentry work. I didn't pick up a hammer. You've got to be carrying shingles, stacking boards, raking the yard, picking up old shingles off the ground, exactly a laborer. They had me cleaning. They had me pulling nails out of boards, stuff like that. . . . Three weeks of doing that. . . . Come to find out, they had the white guy working on the inside work, and then the other inside job just came up last week. They decided it was the first time I was able to pick up a hammer and saw. Re-shingled inside this lady's house. I tore out her mailbox and she loved it.

Mark said that he believed his performance would result in his being called back for the next day to do interior work. Rather than wait for the contractor to call him the following morning, Mark called the man. He said the contractor told him:

"Well, you know, I'm doing some cutting back, I'm going to have to let you go. I'll call you Friday, you can pick your check up. . . ." And [on Friday] he said, "Well, you know, things not picking up. . . ." Then he said, made reference to me not being on time. I said, "I'm not due to be in for an hour," you know. "You know, I'm still in my underclothes. I'm not due to be in. What you mean late?" He said, "Well, now, well, you know, not really so much that, we just cutting back and things be . . . well, it just didn't work out." I said, "Well, do you think it do with me being the only black person to work for you? Because if you're doing cut-backs, did you just hire two people Friday?" You know, "Well, you know, it just didn't work out." I said, "Thanks, man," and I just hung the phone up. And it just, you know, I just sit there for a minute. What just happened, you know? You know, I've had those kind of experiences before, you know.

Mark explained that this reaction was not unfamiliar to him. He went on to share how he was handled during a moment at work when property had apparently been stolen and the guy that was blamed for it was a worker whom Mark had brought into the work opportunity. He said:

Something came up missing. They ran security check on just my company. One of the guys had a misdemeanor shoplifting and the guy [whom Mark had recruited for the job] that was [formerly] in jail, he had had something that had to do with carrying a concealed weapon. So they pulled all of my licenses, took my licenses and fined me a thousand dollars for every hour he worked. And took all my equipment, all the records that I had registered to the company, took all of that. And they said because I wasn't supposed to hire anybody with a felony. I said, "Well, he was subcontracting himself to me for security."

Mark explained that he did not have the resources to conduct background checks on who he brought in to work. However, as the company
was bonded he thought that it would be protected from any losses due to
theft. He continued with his story:

> So what came up missing was a gold-filled ring from out of one of the
> cars that one of the valets parked, and somebody, a lady, lost her credit
> card out of one of the rooms. . . . And he [the supervisor] just ruined
> me, you know, for a minute, you know. And at the same time, I had
> custody of my oldest daughter and my little boy, and my little bitty
> baby girl, and I had no job all of a sudden. Couldn't work, couldn't do
> security work.

Ronald Gregory is a 35-year-old with some community college experience. He has done some maintenance work and some welding. He said:

> I think that when people . . . when African American males come file
> for . . . you know, when they come in and fill out an application, you
> know, they need to be considerate and call back, and don't say, oh,
> well, I give this to the . . . my supervisor and he'll give you a call and
> then I don't hear nothing. You know, like I went to the Crawford Door
> sale, right downtown Ypsi. . . . I popped back in there yesterday. They
> looking all surprised. I was like . . . I was like, "Well, what I really came
> in to get my resume, because I couldn't do it on the computer." So I
> was like, "Well, this is the last place I put it, so I can get a copy." So
> they gave me a copy. And I was like, "Well, you all looked at the
> resume yet?" He was like, "Well . . . we hired somebody right now. We
> try to see how they work out. If they don't work out, then we'll give
> you a call."

This struck Ronald as a common example of not being taken seriously by
a potential employer. He went on to say:

> All I get is disappointed. I had to come back down here for you all to
> say that to me. Why you didn't call me on the phone? You know, I did
> give you the resume. You know, at least call back and say, "Hey, we
> not hiring right now, but, you know, we did look at your resume." I
> don't get none of that stuff. None of that."

In support of this claim, Tracy Barton, a 25-year-old who attended community college and worked for a short while at the University of Michigan in hospital patient care, said:

> White people look out for white people. That's the problem what I have
> with our people, we don't look out for each other, and rather than see

another brother get on top, you know what I'm saying? . . . I think white people have a very good opportunity to get a good job, because they are always looking out for each other. I mean, just look at every workplace that you go into. If it's not black owned, then the white people are the majority in the job, because they are not going to have more blacks there than whites—ever. . . . No matter how much education you get, the white people is always going to be the majority, and they are going to look out for them first. . . . Like, I would be at work at most of my jobs, if the white people aren't doing anything, it's O.K., right? But if I sit back and relax and don't do anything and share with them, it's a problem. You know what I'm saying? Even in my office if my coworker is not doing nothing she is just O.K., this is a chill day, I'm not going to do any work. . . . She doesn't really have to do any work and it's O.K. But if I sit back and relax on my job, I won't have it too long, period. It is as simple as that.

Social interaction across racial lines is common in the everyday lives of black Ypsilantians. Ypsilanti is so small that frequent if not daily encounters with white Americans are a normal part of life. This is important background context for the kind of race talk engaged in by black Ypsilantians. Their talk about race relations came from their experiencing two forms of intimacy. First, they were geographically close to white Americans. Even if the latter did not walk the streets where many black Ypsilantians lived, they did encounter each other in the public spaces of their small city. They also encountered each other at work, where black Ypsilantians usually served in subordinate positions. Hence, black Ypsilantians developed their racial sensibilities out of the unique intimacy afforded to them by their small-city experience.

As I had experienced in researching low-income black men in Chicago, the large-city context can result in some African Americans having little to no sustained cross-racial interaction, such that they struggle to offer precise claims about how they think race may matter in their everyday lives (Young 1999, 2000, 2004). This was not the case for black Ypsilantians. Thus, living in proximity to whiteness meant embracing notions of racial constraint quite unambiguously.

Most of the people featured in this book had some degree of work experience. That experience brought them into contact with white Americans, either as employers, customers, or clients. Unlike the case in larger cities, where some retail establishments are so nested within African American residential communities that nearly the entire clientele is African American, retail work for black Ypsilantians nearly always involved cross-racial interaction because the African American residential communities in that city were never far from majority white areas. Consequently, many of these retail establishments served white Americans as well. This meant that while at work, and working in positions of powerlessness, the black Ypsilantians who held these jobs consistently encountered white Americans, many of whom were of greater privilege. Thus, it was common for black Ypsilantians, many of whom worked as clerical workers, custodians, or service providers in retail sectors, to embrace the notion that they were easily replaceable. When at work they were subjected to cross-racial power differentials that, together with their experiences as lower-tier or marginal workers, provided them with a unique vantage point to comment about the interconnection of race and work.

The three black Ypsilantians in this book who worked in lower-tier administrative positions in Ann Arbor also functioned from subordinate status but had a slightly different vantage point on privilege. Having access to those jobs meant either possessing a skill set or acquiring experience that allowed them slightly more comfort in understanding racial interactive dynamics at work, or at least in not feeling as vulnerable as did those with lesser job experience. Accordingly, most of them had stories to share about the power and effects of racism at work, but they did so with much less of a sense utter despair. Rather than inhibiting success in finding and securing employment, racism was perceived by them as a major inconvenience in the workplace.

CONCLUSION

The general pattern of work history that black Ypsilantians have experienced contributes to a particular manner of talking about the world of work and work opportunity. That is, the great majority of these people have had a variety of lower-tier work experiences. Rather than being able to launch or build careers, they have most often just been in and out of work. In fact, a major theme that seemed to run throughout the interviews is that people will have many jobs in their lifetimes. Therefore, momentary discord with coworkers and starting off at a job that is not a passion are minor issues. If these become consistent, they are setbacks.

Black Ypsilantians had much to say about the structure of Ypsilanti's world of work and how one could best manage that environment. They all spoke quite extensively about what that world could offer them and what they wanted to acquire from it. There also was a strong emphasis on achieving satisfaction with one's work rather than with the status of one's job. The reason is that the kind of work they have most often done brings little material or emotional satisfaction. Hence, work for them has not been about finding fulfillment but simply about allowing them to make ends meet. The consequence of such experiences is that work is talked about as a means to an end rather than an end in and of itself. This distinction is a key one that separates the experiences of many white-collar professionals from those who have worked in semi- or minimally skilled blue-collar sectors.

The black Ypsilantians in this book were interviewed at a time when memories of security and durability in work remained among the oldest of them. The youngest had heard about such security and durability as stories were passed down over time. Hence their commentary about work is riddled with anxiety because of the particular historical backdrop undergirding it. Black Ypsilantians drew clear distinctions between the types of jobs that they saw as available and the types of jobs that they believed would allow them to meet their needs and interests. Even if the past few decades had been near the tail end of the expansive mobility possibilities made available by the automobile industry, they had grown up in a region where automobile manufacturing was the source of the still-predominant images of good work. The work itself was not glamorous, but it was stable and rewarding. Most important, it represented a historic image of a career to black Ypsilantians. The significance of this is that African Americans in that city continued to maintain a strong sense of the value of a career rather than the mere possession of a job. This must be kept in mind as we turn to how they talked about what good work means to them and what they believe stands in the way of getting such work in their lives.

NOTES

1. The critical attitude toward fast-food employment, especially given that a number of the men had had or at the time of the interviews still had employment in this arena, contrasts with Katherine Newman's (2000) portrayal of the perceived utility of fast-food jobs in her study *Ain't No Shame in My Game*. A major part of the difference in

outlook between these men and the subjects of Newman's work is that she focused on a slightly younger cohort of individuals, who saw these jobs as crucial first steps in a long-term plan for upward mobility. The people in my analysis saw these jobs as dead-end positions that did not connect in any meaningful way to the kinds of employment that they hoped to attain in a much more immediate future.

2. While Ypsilanti is home to Eastern Michigan University (student population of 20,000), it does not have the research and technology infrastructure of the University of Michigan. Accordingly, its reputation is significantly more grounded in serving the local community. Interestingly, the institution did not surface in discussions of job prospects for black Ypsilantians, nor did more than a few of them mention it as an option for further education. As EMU sits on the northern boundary of the city (separated from much of the rest of the city by a major boulevard that is not inviting for pedestrian traffic), it does not serve as a conduit through the city. Although it is largely a commuter institution, student housing surrounds the campus, and the southern portion of that housing is more than a comfortable walk from where most of the black Ypsilantians in this book reside. Therefore, campus space is almost wholly occupied by students, staff, and faculty, and not so much by city residents who have no formal membership in those categories.

3. The evidence for this claim rests in careful documentation of the racial and ethnic backgrounds of the friends, family members, and associates for each of the people in this book. These points of contact were documented during the interviews. The study on which this book is based included documentation of the extent to which friends, family members, and associates were reported to have worked in various occupational sectors ranging from unemployed to white-collar professional, to have achieved various levels of educational attainment, and to have experienced other pivotal life conditions (incarceration, involvement in criminal activity, etc.).

Part II

Fitting into the Postindustrial World

FOUR

Imagining the Good Job in a City on the Edge

A deeper dive into how black Ypsilantians envision the good job offers a more thorough account of how they think of the best kind of work options for people like themselves. Their accounts are built from life experiences in jobs that, at least in most cases, did not satisfy them. Accordingly, for them the good job is an idea—an imaginative construct—more than an actual experience. Some may surmise that the depths of the challenges, disappointments, and frustrations that comprise the work experiences of black Ypsilantians might negate any need to attend to what they merely imagine to be good jobs. However, considering their envisioning of jobs that may be beyond their reach, or that may not even exist, informs how they conceive of opportunity.

In order to understand how black Ypsilantians make sense of work and work opportunity in their city, much more must be brought into consideration than what kinds of work they have done or are currently doing and how they feel about their work. This effort must include elucidating the kinds of work they desire and why they do so. It also requires attending to how they situate these interests within broader visions of work opportunity and possibility. Thus, looking at how they construct work-related desires and interests as part of their vision of good jobs allows for learning much about how they understand possibilities for moving from where they are to where they hope to be. It also means moving from how they discussed their past experiences in the world of work to how they envision possible futures in it.

103

Ultimately, what black Ypsilantians want can only be understood by gaining purchase on how they understand the nature of work opportunity. To understand what they want and hope for requires understanding what they think exists and why they think it does. This is foundational for understanding what they conceive of as the best possible kinds of employment prospects for themselves. What is also foundational is that they reside in a small city where the pinnacle of great work and great opportunity rested in the factory. Accordingly, such work is central to what they maintain is the best kind of work available for them. Even if such work is not argued to be in the factory (although for several men, at least, that argument still endures), what else they imagine is built from an image of the factory as the historic source of success and opportunity for the prior generations of black Ypsilantians.

Before embarking on a more thorough consideration of the good job, it must be noted that the importance of understanding their thoughts about good jobs rests not so much in the actual occupations that they report. It is the content of such a discussion and the manner in which they express it that most matters. That content reveals much about how they see themselves as participants in the world of work. Their views of the good job tell about their potential to understand different kinds of work opportunity, which sheds light on how they may respond to what could happen to them in the future. Essentially, addressing this matter reveals how the imagination operates as a muscle for possible future-oriented action. In this chapter I begin to document how expansive the imagination is about good jobs and how much being in Ypsilanti matters for that outcome. Moreover, as we shall see, exploring how black Ypsilantians grasp and grapple with notions of the good job reveals how much gender matters in their thinking about opportunity and possibility in the world of work.

DEFINING THE GOOD JOB

The effort to make sense of how black Ypsilantians conceived of good jobs involved the same comparative analyses (men compared to women, age-group comparisons, parents compared to nonparents, comparisons across educational status levels, etc.) applied to the other issues in this book. That being said, there were many common characteristics in what black Ypsilantians defined as a good job. At a base level, they argued that a good job provides high earnings. Black Ypsilantians did not suggest a common dollar amount as reflective of an acceptable wage. However, the great majority of them said that minimum wage would not suffice (which was $5.15 throughout much of the period in which this research was done, and which stood at $6.86 in 2019). Their emphasis was on work that provided a sense of security and comfort with whatever wages were earned more than on a finite salary.

Ultimately, the foundation of their vision of the good job rested in a comfortable salary, opportunities for raises and advancement, fringe benefits, autonomy, and a sense that the work being done was dignified (either as conveyed by coworkers, bosses, clients, and customers or as cultivated internally by one's reaction to his or her work). Black Ypsilantians also desired work that provided fringe benefits, such as health insurance and retirement plans. They also expressed a value for work that enabled workers to achieve some measure of autonomy and control over work activities.

These conditions are what often give workers a sense of flexibility and control in their work lives (Kalleberg 2011, 9). These characteristics also facilitate another key dimension of the good job: its deliverance of a sense of dignity. As sociologist Arne Kalleberg argues, dignity at work is achieved through a worker's taking pride in his or her productive accomplishments, even if those accomplishments are perceived as modest by an outsider's estimation (Hodson 2001, 4). It is at the core of whether and how workers feel valued at work, of the extent to which they feel alienated or exploited, and of how much regard they have for their actual places of work (Hodson 2001, 22–29).

Carmen Granderson offered an example of this highly common way of thinking. She considers a good job to be one at which she would receive health care and other benefits. The opportunity for advancement or promotion and the hours and flexibility are both important to Carmen. An accessible location and the quality of the workplace environment are also important to her. She said:

> You know, the good paying job with benefits and stuff like that. Because around here like my one friend, she's been working at Wendy's for like four years, and Wendy's doesn't offer any medical benefits, no kind of 401K, nothing. Like you've been working there for four years and it's like you're not going anywhere. She hasn't even got a raise.

In support of this opinion, Oscar Orenthal, a 22-year-old high school graduate who has worked in fast-food services and as a movie theater attendant, said:

> I'm going to go with healthcare benefits (in defining what makes for a good job) because you never know. You could be 19 to 26 and have a heart attack on your job and you ain't got no healthcare benefits or no insurance, whose going to pay for it? So, you got to get a good job that has benefits. . . . Salary . . . it's always good to have a good paying job. . . . Opportunities for promotion, that's just being a good worker. Showing improvement or showing what you're doing around the job, letting your supervisors know, managers, whoever hired you, letting them know that you've got the flexibility and I want a promotion.

These accounts of the attributes of a good job were consistent with those of other black Ypsilantians. Across the board, great value was placed on health and other fringe benefits as attributes of good jobs (66% of nonparents, 77% of parents, 82% of women, 73% of men, 85% of those who attended college for at least a semester, 65% of high school graduates, and 66% of those who did not complete high school all named access to fringe benefits as the most significant aspect of a good job). Salary was the second most mentioned attribute. Those in each of the subgroups regarded its importance at rates of between 55% and 80%. While only 40% of those without a high school diploma or GED mentioned salary as important, they also were preoccupied with the quality of the work experience, itself, as constituting a good job. Women then emphasized flexibility in working hours (71%), a consequence of their being more likely to take account of childcare interests when asked to define the attributes of a good job, while the men then mentioned opportunities for promotion or upward mobility (51%) as the next important attribute. The next common referents were the geographic location of the job and the quality of relationships with coworkers.

These findings do not differ from other accounts of what people in the Midwestern industrial sphere conceive of as good work (Young 2000; Hamer 2001; Silva 2013; Dudley 1994). According to the literature, the ideal was work that allowed workers to use their hands, produce or create a tangible product, get paid a decent wage, and receive fringe benefits that could provide them with protection in case of injuries.

Geri Benton, who was unemployed at the time of her interview, put it as follows:

Well, probably one [of] the most important ones to me would be the flexibility of hours and healthcare benefits. Those probably would be the most. Because, by me having three kids, you know, it's really hard to find a job during the day when the kids are at school. And, then it's really hard, being a single parent, maintaining three boys, and then you're working until nighttime and they're in bed by the time you get home. So, I can work some afternoons, but not every day afternoons, because I still have to raise these kids I have. And, other than that, what did I say healthcare benefits? Well, one of my sons has asthma, so therefore I have to make sure, so when I take him to the doctor, we ain't talking about no $1,000 doctor bill that I can't pay.

Several others made similar points:

Well, one [job] that you can have a future with. That you could . . . enough to say, to put some money up every time you get paid and enough to pay all your bills and still have some left over. (Brock Bevins)

Well, a place that you feel good that you know . . . you doing your work you have to do and you feel proud of yourself and where you feel like you making an accomplishment. You know what I'm talking about? You feel like you making a difference. Something that . . . a job that makes you feel good about yourself and what you're doing. (Eric Ellison, age 31)

You know, I like the job that will advance you. That'll give you an opportunity to be successful at something else, not just keep you at the same that you walked in at. You know? (Sabel Janis)

Much more common for the women was discussion of family-friendly work opportunities as constituting a good job. In expressing her views on the matter, Karen Andrews said:

A lot of jobs, it needs to be more family oriented. . . . They need to be more helpful towards parents, you know, people with kids. Especially single parents, because there's so many of us out here, you know, that don't have kids with 'em. So they need to be more compassionate and they need to, you know, find out what the needs are for their employees. Such as people, you know, singles coming in with, you know, single families and stuff like that. And then I think it'll be much better because it's like issues like the child care and you know, the attendance, and stuff like that. That all revolves around family. So they need to work on those type of issues.

Another issue brought up by many was the importance of doing a job that one intrinsically liked and desired to do. It was also important that the job garnered the respect of others. Larry Lawson, a high school graduate who has been a custodian and a temporary clerical worker, added:

> I mean, you can make, you know, your job can pay top dollar, you know what I'm saying? But, if it's something where you got to work eight hours that you don't enjoy, eventually, you ain't going to be there long, you know? It's got to be something that you enjoy doing, you know what I'm saying? It's got to be something that you enjoy doing. I can understand getting a job you don't enjoy doing so while you working at that job you stay looking for other employment, you know what I'm saying? But, it's nothing like having a job that you're not happy at, you know? Nothing like that.

Larry also said the following about the qualities of good jobs:

> You know, when somebody is like, "Where you work at?" and you tell somebody you working at like the post office or something like that, or you working at the VA or the federal prison, or you tell somebody you working at the plant. They'll be like, "Man, dude making some loot." This is just the standout about the job. If you tell somebody, you know, they're like, "Where you work at," and you say, "I work at the White Castle." They're like, "Pssh." You know? You know what I mean? Slipping on grease all day, man, for minimum wage.

Notions of the good job were rooted in what it delivered in terms of both material and status rewards. The material rewards included salary and fringe benefits, and the status rewards involved how the job enabled people to feel good about their work and to register a sense that others were impressed by the kind of work they did. The major gender-specific quality was flexibility, which women emphasized to a much greater extent than did the men.

The Bad Job

A part of every discussion of good jobs involved ascertaining the qualities of bad jobs. As black Ypsilantians claimed much more experience with unfulfilling jobs, their discussion of good jobs was made complete by what they defined as bad ones. Not surprisingly, black Ypsilantians stated that bad jobs pay low wages and do not lead to higher wages over time. They do not provide fringe benefits and do not enable workers to exert control over the work activities. They do not provide a worker with flexibility to deal with nonwork issues (Kalleberg 2011, 10). These were jobs that were short term, such as handing out flyers or running errands for local merchants, or otherwise paid low wages, which for these individuals meant jobs at or near the minimum wage. The rationale for not accepting work that did not pay what they believed was an acceptable wage was that there were ways of making that income without having to report to a job that provided a taxable income. As Karen Andrews said in discussing minimum wage jobs:

> I think it's $5.25 [in the year 2000]. And hell no. I will not [accept that.] . . . I will pick up some cans all day [instead]. I would. I ain't taking $5.00. . . . I know I can get something better than $5.00. I mean, if I was 14, and I didn't have a family and bills, you know, $5.00 is a lot of money. I mean, a $200.00 check is a lot of money when you're 12 and you ain't got shit to do with it. But, come on. Now you can't do it.

Karen took a brief pause to reflect, then said:

> I ain't going to say never . . . 'cause a check is better than no check. But no, uh. . . . Some employers know that there's people out there with not many skills that will settle for that, because nobody else would hire them. So it's always going to be people out there with . . . who didn't graduate from college, who didn't graduate from high school, who don't know how to read real good, who don't know how to write real good . . . .that they can get for $5.50, and some people that settle for that, 'cause they feel like that's all they can do.

Brian Fuller made the same argument about minimum wage jobs:

> I won't work for minimum wage. Not like that. . . . As long as there's temp services around, I would get another one [job]. I mean, I've got a custodial certificate, doing carpet, you know, cleaning upholstery, buffing and waxing . . . stripping. Probably if I tried to find something like that, I might be able to [get another job].

The generic qualities of the good job revealed little that should surprise. Salary, fringe benefits, and the opportunity for promotion and career advancement were attributes that were widely shared, along with a work environment that was vacant of extreme social turbulence and animosity. As evident in the portrait of work histories provided in the appendix, what black Ypsilantians say they will not accept and what they have accepted in terms of work are somewhat at odds. Thus, their reporting of what they will not accept serves little utility as statement of fact. It does serve as an important source of understanding their desires and interests concerning the world of work. Accordingly, a critical assessment of what they say in this chapter does not depict what kinds of work they may ultimately do in the future but rather what they want from work, especially from what they conceive of as good jobs. In continuing this investigation into the good job, we next turn to gender-specific commentary. To understand why such a divide existed for black Ypsilantians, one must acknowledge that even though the factory loomed large in reflections about a better time for work in Ypsilanti, the very form of work done there was traditionally performed by men.

GENDER DIVIDES IN CONCEPTUALIZING THE GOOD JOB

Crucial gender distinctions emerged when black Ypsilantians were asked for actual examples of good jobs. Again, this discussion did not emerge organically, as respondents initially directed the conversation to the qualities of good jobs and not specific types. To complete this part of the inquiry, however, they were asked to define what kinds of jobs struck them as good. Unlike the men, women were not nearly as invested in good work, past or future, as being located in a manufacturing or factory setting. Even if women recognized the historic importance of the automobile manufacturing industry for labor in Ypsilanti, it was seen by them as the kind of work mostly done by men. Consequently, women did not feel that the closure of the factory resulted in a personal loss of meaningful work opportunity. This uniquely situated the women in terms of envisioning places for themselves in the postindustrial era. As we will see, for the men the end of the factory was both a community-level loss and a personal one because it was a common reference for their notion of good jobs.

The Women

Jenita Yvette is 27 years old. She has worked as a self-employed childcare attendant, as a housecleaner, and in retail security. She has five children and has attended some community college. Jenita's ideal job is in health care because she enjoys the work and the ability to help others. She believes that enjoying the job is important and that it isn't always about the money. Benefits are also important for Jenita. She said:

> I have a heart for helping people who can't help themselves and who need help and are sometimes ashamed or uncomfortable. I mean . . . you're dealing with some system, you're dealing with somebody that's down and out, can't work, can't walk, can't clean your body properly, along those lines. They need someone.

The women's sense of good jobs was rooted in discussions of service work, or what can be labeled "pink-collar" employment. Included here were cleaning, nursing, service work in hospitals or nursing homes, teaching, and social or clerical work. In making their cases, they said that the virtue of this kind of work is that it allowed them to both help other people and learn new skills. In essence, the women emphasized their passion for helping others and in doing so discussed acquiring more formal education as essential for obtaining their ideal jobs. The women also were more inclined to discuss the good job as allowing one to have personal connections with clients or customers, thus indicating that they desired not simply service work, but specific types of such work that they could readily identify as personally rewarding.

For example, we turn to Cherry Robards. She was 34 years old and unemployed when interviewed. She has worked as a laundry attendant at the University of Michigan hospital. She is a divorced mother of two. Her ultimate goal is to become a special education teacher. She believes that a good job is one in which the individual enjoys the work, and that this is more important than the pay one receives. Health-care benefits, the relationship with supervisors and coworkers, and the opportunity for mobility or promotion are important to her as well. She said:

> I liked that job because I worked with a lot of kids that didn't have all their basic skills, and it's really exciting and really rewarding when you start working with a student that was a D student and in two months' time, or the end of the next marking period, you've brought this student up to a B average and you see this student light up and come to live and grow.

Barbara Champion is 39 years old and unemployed. She has worked in patient care. She has four children and is separated from her husband. She lives in a household with many extended family members. She has attended community college without completing a degree. Barbara desires to be a social worker and wants jobs that "serve purpose" for her. Also, the work environment, salary, benefits, and hours are important aspects of a good job for her. Hours and flexibility, location, relationships with supervisors and coworkers, opportunity for promotion, and union membership are all important to Barbara. She said:

> To be able to work at a safe house [a facility providing temporary housing and services to physically abused women and their children], uh, my um because of my experience. I would get much gratification for doing something like that because I know about domestic violence and all the things that go along with it, and if I could just say something to help somebody along the way, I would like that.

The women's ideas of good work had a lot to do with feeling good about themselves as a consequence of what they believed they were offering to others in the course of their work. They expressed that they felt good about themselves when they were helping or working with others. For instance, Lanice Daniels, age 39, argued that becoming a bus driver would fulfill her pursuit of a good job because that kind of work would allow her to work with children. She said:

> I babysitted children. My next door neighbor's kids. That kept a little income coming in for me. And then I kind of moved up in the school system. I did some daycare at the school daycare, then I did a program where the grandparents come in and show skills, I was coordinator over that. And then something caught my eye, and that was the school bus. And that's what I wanted to do. Traveling and then I'm still with my children. You know, like sometime I take 'em on field trips. I would try to use my license. Like I say, but that might stop me right now because the points, but anyway, besides that, I would use my license work for me. Factory work is always out there. I would like to get in the factory for the money, assembly. You know, the light industrial type of work.

In another case of emphasizing the social relational dimensions of work, Lena Antonio, age 25, spoke of her desire to become a social worker. She said:

> My idea of a good job would be a job where you feel comfortable. A job where you know that, you know, you're going in here, you're making a difference. Because you know you're going in here and making a difference, it keeps you motivated to come back, because you want to see your employment status progress. You want to see the people you work around progress. You want to see if you're working with clients or what have you, you want to see them progress and in my opinion that's like quality number one is that you're comfortable with doing it and the people around you are receiving something beneficial from it.

Tracy Barton explained that teaching would provide her with the most fulfillment:

> My ideal job is one where, something that I enjoy doing. . . . Something I enjoy doing and I'm happy getting up in the morning, you know, doing my job, going to work every day. I think I would be happy teaching. . . . The hours are nice, you know what I'm saying? I love kids, I love people, you know, and I really want to see students get ahead, you know.

Ann Marie Davis, age 31, talked about a career in personal care:

> To have a job that I enjoy [is a good job], although the pay don't hurt, but as long as I like doing it, you know. Because I could be making way more than I'm making working in a hospital somewhere but it's just ain't what I want to do. I like more of that personal kind of care, where you can get to know people. And not just that, oh she's in the hospital for two days and now she's gone, you know. . . . I love taking care of people.

To be clear, Ypsilanti's history of rewarding factory-based work was not lost on the women, even if few of them actually desired that kind of work for themselves. To convey the unique way in which the factory mattered for many women, we turn to the case of Sabel Janis. Again, she was 31 years old when interviewed and was unemployed even though she had worked as a clerical worker in a temporary capacity, and she has three children. Sabel believes the opportunity for promotion is important for jobs. She also desires a job that she would enjoy and that would pay well. Unlike most of the other women, she was quite specific about the salary demarcations of a good job. At the time she was interviewed she said that she would work for no less than $9.50 an hour (the equivalent of about $14.50 in 2019).

Recall that Sabel's mother and stepfather, and several extended family members, had all worked in Ford Motor Company plants. Her knowledge of the history of her family's work experience is where she got her ideas about what constitutes a good job. However, assembly line work was not what she found appealing. For Sabel, the factory was central not because it represented the kind of job that she desired, but because the kind of remuneration and benefits that came with it were central in what she imagined that she wanted from a good job. She also settled on an image of a good job, a desk job, which contained attributes that starkly contrasted with what she found distasteful about the automobile factory.

This is yet another way in which the factory mattered even for women who did not envision themselves actually working on a shop floor.

As for the other black Ypsilantians, male and female, health-care benefits, hours and flexibility, location, relationship with supervisors and co-workers, and union membership were important for Sabel. Moreover, she said, "I like the job that will advance you. That'll give you an opportunity to be successful at something else, not just keep you at the same that you walked in at."

Along those same lines, Karen Andrews explained that she wanted to work in an office setting that would allow her to receive a good salary, but more important, that would enable her to work in a capacity that permitted her to help people solve their personal problems. She said:

> It's got to be offering me some money. So that could be computers, because I done went to school for computers at the college, Washtenaw [community college.] . . . So that can be from anything like that to being an advisor or counseling young people who, you know . . . who's not there yet. You know, 12, 13, 14, because at them ages, you know, by the time I was 20, I had three kids. You understand what I'm saying? So I want to catch 'em before that and let 'em know [about what to do better with their lives] so, I'd like to deal with young people or something like that.

Unlike the men, the majority of the women often argued that a good job was one that allowed for investing in quality family time. They rarely talked about work as disassociated from family concerns. What is most revealing, however, is the extent to which the women talked about good jobs as rooted in providing some form of service to others. Furthermore, women discussed the value of the primarily pink-collar jobs available. They were motivated to work in such environments because they believed such opportunities would bolster self-esteem, sense of responsibility, and independence in the manner they most desired. Essentially, for women, good jobs involved opportunities to invest in the kind of relational dynamics highly associated with certain service-sector jobs.

The Men

Aside from the general attributes discussed previously, the men's discussions of the good job focused on work that garnered respect. Unlike the women, who emphasized the relational dimensions of work, the men were more disposed to emphasize the identity characteristics of work.

Put another way, while women spoke of how good jobs allowed them to serve others, men were more inclined to speak about good jobs in terms of what possessing them did for their self-identity and feelings of self-worth.

Ralph Remington, a 21-year-old who has taken some community college courses and has done some day laboring in construction, explained:

> A good job? When you can go home, you know what I'm saying, and your body feeling tight, sore, you know what I'm saying? That's a good job to me. Getting in the plant. . . . To be in a shirt and pants and have oil all over me, you know. . . . I would just feel real good about it. . . . And, you going to run into people, you know, and they going to be looking at you like, you know, "He work hard," you know what I'm saying? That's the type of stuff that I like to see.

Emphasizing another kind of blue-collar opportunity, Carl Fulton explained that he imagines working in a small apartment complex that he would also own, thus allowing him complete freedom of control at work and immediate access to his family. This would allow him to maximize the joys of work and home life. In order to make his dream become reality, he wants to remain in construction or physical plant care, as those are the fields that he feels he is best suited for. As he said:

> I like the maintenance field. . . . The great jobs are the ones to where you can get up in the morning and it doesn't feel like a job. You just feel like, oh, I gotta go in and take care of this. Like working for . . . working for the apartment complex where I live. This don't feel like a job to me.

He continued:

> Uh, once I get my four-unit apartment building, I'm through. I'm not gonna work [for anybody else] no more. After I get these four units, I'm gonna live in one and rent out the other three and then I'm gonna go look for some more property. I'll be my own maintenance man and own management staff and I am gonna be through.

As is the case for so many other Americans, what stands in the way of Carl achieving his dream is debt and opportunity. He said, "I'm like about ten grand in debt right now. And I haven't been able to pay off any of it because I'm so busy trying to make money to survive. And take care of my family and of myself." Realizing his constraints, Carl said that he is willing to settle for a job that will allow him to have some control over his hours and some access to his children. As he put it:

I like what I'm doing now. I don't even want to work full time. But if um, if a maintenance job happened to come up for that twelve, fifteen dollars an hour, I'm not, I'm not gonna turn it down. I'm not really looking for a job. . . . Right now I just want to work the least amount of hours that I can. That sounds really sick [but] I want to spend more time with my family. . . . I want some more children.

What the men desired was secure blue-collar work that affirmed their physical capabilities. They wanted to be in automobile plants, in factories, or behind the wheels of trucks. Some wanted to be security guards or officers. They often discussed job security and salary as indicators of good jobs. A great irony in the men's discussions, however, was that many of them mentioned how their labor could be exploited, even in good jobs. To counter this prevailing concern, the good job for them also meant the opportunity to become business owners or serve as supervisors or be promoted. Again, a core characteristics of this interest was how it garnered respect.

Mention of achieving respect and garnering workplace status was much more common in the commentary of the men. For instance, we now turn to 19-year-old Desmond James, who dropped out of high school, is unemployed, and lives with his child. He desires a place where he can feel respected and can get the hours he wants. He also prefers a job that he would enjoy over one for which he would get paid a lot. Health care and benefits, hours and flexibility, location, relationships with supervisor and coworkers, salary, opportunity for promotion, and union membership are all important aspects of a job for him. Desmond said, "Somewhere where you get respect and you can just work, you know, the hours that you *need to*."

Rick Darnett was 30 years old and unemployed when interviewed. He has been a public school teacher's aide and, after being fired from that job, a store clerk. He is a high school graduate, and he lives with his girlfriend and their two children. As he put it, "To me, it make me less than a man. I mean, I just don't feel right. When I walk in there, I want to turn back around. I went into McDonald's, and I got right there and I had to stop and say, 'I can't work at McDonald's.'"

Geoff Jerguson was 32 years old when interviewed. He was unemployed and the father of a child who resided in the mother's home. He had not completed high school but had worked in janitorial services. For Geoff, a good job is one that would allow him to work independently and even with a team if necessary. He prioritizes a job that he would enjoy over the pay he would receive. He said, "I mean, any job that you could do with dignity and with a sufficient amount of pay, you know, that you enjoy to do would be something good for you."

Reese Jersey was 21 years old when interviewed. He worked as a day laborer at construction sites. He lived with a roommate and had one child. He had some community college experience. Reese's idea of a good job would be one that pays well and has a pleasant work environment. Also, a job that he could be proud of and respected for is important to him, as are health-care benefits, hours and flexibility, salary, opportunity for promotion, and union membership. He said:

> Working at ESPN, you know, something like that, just a high profile job. A job where I could say, "Hey, I work at ESPN," or "I work at Channel Four." Something that, you know, people ask me about and then I'm not, you know, ashamed to say I work there and I look forward to, you know, just going to work and meeting new people.

Finally, Brian Fuller's notion of a good job was one that would allow him to be financially secure and the owner of his own home. While earlier we learned that achieving family stability was his utmost goal given the situation that he was experiencing with his children, he also said:

> I want to own a house. And I got a goal. I want to have like [a] landscaping-lawn care business, snow removal thing. But I just can't do right now. I'm going through too much stuff and . . . I'm not really sure yet, because I mean, like I said, we're right behind our goals and stuff, but once we get everything paid up, everything situated, you know, because she's got a bank account. Put some money away. I'm going to talk to my brother, see if . . . because he also wanted to . . . he was thinking about getting into the lawn care thing.

The previous remarks are examples of how almost every man talked about work from the perspective of desiring greater autonomy. Many wanted to become their own bosses. They wanted fair pay. Most important, they sought an opportunity to claim pride, dignity, respect, and what they regarded as virtuous manhood. This aligns with what many low-income and working-class men, white or black, desire (Kimmel 1996; Simpson, Hughes, and Slutskaya 2016; Ackers 2014; Crowley 2013; Baron 2006; Rotundo 1993; Schrock and Schwalbe 2009; Acker 1990; Collinson 1992; Wacquant 2003).

The men often talked about what the good job would do for their sense of personal identity in ways that would not de-emphasize service to others, but rather provide elevated attention to social status and individual accomplishments made at work. For them, good jobs were the kind that involved affirming individualistic attributes (work-related accomplishments and the personal status affirmations that come from certain jobs). They discussed manual labor jobs as demeaning experiences from which they would rather dissociate. By and large, the work they experienced did not strengthen their sense of autonomy or their sense of manhood. A corrective to this is what they sought from good jobs.

CONCLUSION: THE SAID AND UNSAID ABOUT THE GOOD JOB

Black Ypsilantians' discussions of good jobs were set within their being caught in a world of deprivation, in terms of both their families' material situations and the social environment circumscribing their lives. The kinds of jobs that not only were sought after, but also were regarded as essential if family stability and security were going to be achieved, were those most plentiful in a bygone era in Ypsilanti—the kinds with fringe benefits and union membership. The kinds of jobs that they believed were easily accessible provided minimal material reward, little job security, and no fringe support.

For black Ypsilantians the good job is primarily about financial stability, but it also is about so much more. It is about being able to validate oneself as a parent for those who have children or who desire to do so in the future. Yet that validation takes on gendered forms. Many of the women find validation in being with their children and engaging in their children's development. Many of the men find validation in being financial supporters of their children.

Women's comments revealed that they want skilled, professional jobs that impact the community, as this would allow them to feel good about themselves. Many women discussed getting an education in order to obtain work as a nurse, social worker, or secretary. Men discussed factory work, truck driving, and officer or guard positions as good jobs. But ideally, the majority of men mentioned factors having to do with personal or social identity. The content of their discussion of the good job centered much more on what the job would do for their sense of self than what it would do for others, even if their notion of the good job involves service to others.

While men were less likely than women to discuss their career goals, they were explicit in stating that they were tired of their labor being exploited at blue-collar jobs and therefore desired work that not only was financially secure but also would grant more autonomy. Women are able to make meaning out of pink-collar jobs because they find it meaningful to help and work with people, especially people in the community.

In contrast, men just find blue-collar work exploitative, even if they also find it to be rewarding in terms of allowing them to make effective use of their bodies, so they talked more about feeling exploited. Some men mentioned helping the community or working with family, or discussed their non-blue-collar dream jobs, such as becoming a doctor. But by and large, more women talked about their family, talents, and passion for helping others.

Ultimately, very few black Ypsilantians discussed white-collar work as their idea of the good job. Again, this reflects a distancing from the kinds of more prominent work found in neighboring Ann Arbor. Instead, much of the discussion centered on working-class jobs available in the area. Most everyone desired jobs that had stable pay as opposed to ones that would provide disposable income. Most everyone also agreed that having a job one enjoys is more important than having a higher paying job, although women were more emphatic about this than men.

FIVE

The Work Ethic in Principle and in Practice

I'll do my job. And if I see a person need help, I'll step up without somebody saying help him. I'll go help him, you know. (Jerry Jackson)

This guy challenged me [at work]. He said you don't move fast enough. I said you're not paying enough. I just told him just like that. I said, "You pay me more." You get what you pay for, you know. (Jerry Jackson)

At first glance, these two statements make Jerry Jackson seem like a contradiction. However, there is more to him than is apparent in these statements. Jerry was introduced in the first chapter. Recall that he is a 42-year-old man who has been unemployed for most of his adult life. When he was working, he did so as a custodian at an automobile plant. When asked to explain his work ethic, Jerry provided the first response. In it he suggested that he does his job and that without being asked he would go the extra yard for someone who appears to be struggling while at work alongside him. A few minutes later, when asked about whether anyone has challenged his work ethic, he provided the second response. There he talked about being challenged when working at the plant for not performing at an optimal level, and he was quite clear in explaining precisely why this was the case. It may seem like enough to say that Jerry Jackson, and many of the other people featured in this book, know how to deliver the right message about possessing a good work ethic but cannot deliver on it when explaining their behavior at work. This understanding, however, is far too incomplete.

Jerry Jackson is not a contradiction, nor are the people in this book who spoke about work experiences in a similar manner. Instead, these remarks elucidate the kind of vantage point black Ypsilantians maintain about their orientation to jobs that they do not find rewarding. To paraphrase anthropologist Elliot Liebow in his 1960 classic *Tally's Corner*, a study of street corner men in Washington, D.C. (most of whom held jobs despite their propensity for spending free time on the street corner), the kind of jobs that Jerry Jackson and other black Ypsilantians held delivered little and promised no more (Liebow 1967, 63). Liebow also said that street corner men who are engaged in this kind of work put no lower value on the job than does the larger society around them (57). Hence, the men in Liebow's book often worked in a cavalier fashion, as if all that mattered was the immediate satisfaction of present appetites and the surrender to present moods (63–64).

What Liebow said over 50 years ago applies to many of the men and women in this book. His statements also undergird the focus of this chapter, which unpacks the complexities in how black Ypsilantians talk about their work ethic. Here we explore the inner thoughts of black Ypsilantians about how they envision approaching the modern world of work. We examine their self-inventory of work-related skills—what others might call human capital, or the physical and mental capacities to get work done (Coleman 1988)—and the dispositions (attitudes, values, etc.) that they believe they bring to the world of work. It is important to pay attention to these dimensions of the work ethic because they assist in gaining purchase on how black Ypsilantians make sense of their immersion into a precarious and unfulfilling world of work. The following pages move beyond a trite listing of traits and characteristics that are commonly associated with a work ethic (working hard, being timely, commitment, etc.). Instead, the effort here is to draw attention to the narrative patterns constructed by black Ypsilantians as they talk about their ethic. It is in those patterns that a more evocative sense of how they imagine their response to work emerges. Indeed, therein lies the kind of work-related character they have constructed, which is one that claims to get the job done but does not want to be abused or debased while on the job. This is a core part of what I refer to as their *functional selves*.

The functional self emerges in response to a pervasive public perception of disadvantaged people as stuck in place, a concept drawn from the work of sociologist Patrick Sharkey (2013) in his analysis of the lives of the urban poor. The sense that the disadvantaged are stuck in place is rooted in the public image of the African American poor as either unable or unwilling to improve upon their life situation. Hence, the ways in which they talk about their work ethic, even if they sound similar to the way in which more secure people may articulate the concept, are motivated by the particular station that the disadvantaged are locked into in the American public imagination. The concept of the functional self refers to an individual's vision of what she or he can offer to the modern world of work such that status as a "worthy" social being can be acknowledged over and against what happens to be her or his actual work status.

The functional self is not intended to offer an entirely new intellectual portrait of human behavior or individual consciousness. Indeed, there have been many debates about the notion of the self that have taken up these and other issues pertaining to how people come to recognize and explain to others their self of individuality, particularity, or uniqueness in the social world (Burkitt 2008; Callero 2003; Gergen 2000; Giddens 1991; Holstein and Gubrium 2000; Stets and Carter 2011). Instead, my point about the functional self is that it acknowledges how one comes to terms with living in confining and constraining circumstances without appearing to be incapable or inadequate (to oneself as well as to others). The functional self is foundational to the kind of narrative that disenfranchised people provide to challenge that depiction.

In exploring how black Ypsilantians portray functional selves, this chapter also draws upon the concept of the *conarrative* to help make sense of what may strike one as seemingly contradictory claims, such as the kind offered by Jerry at the start of this chapter. A conarrative is a concept suggested by educational sociologist Carla O'Connor (1997) to explain how people blend dominant narratives with alternative or modifying claims about social reality. Conarratives help interpret why and how some people adhere to what many take to be standard notions or ideas about social life, but (often due to their status as disadvantaged, marginal, or subordinate in some way) also offer modifications, enriched interpretations, or caveats and conditionals to dominant narratives. Essentially, then, a conarrative creates a space for those who do not wholly reject normative arguments, but who believe that something more than the normative perspective is necessary for explicating their vision of themselves or of social reality.

Consider, for example, what many regard to be the dominant narrative of socioeconomic mobility in America (what I explore later in this chapter as the work ethic in principle): a commitment to hard work, determination, and the possession of proper skills and credentials. A *counternarrative* would be that mobility is universally controlled and regulated by the elite, and that others must simply follow the rules for mobility that the most privileged have created. This reflects a wholesale rejection of the dominant narrative. The alternative of concern here, a conarrative, would consist of the dominant narrative (composed of hard work, determination, and the possession of skills and credentials) supplemented with an emphasis on having the right kinds of social connections, luck, status in an a priori privileged category (white, male, etc.), or some other condition or factor that is not incorporated into the dominant narrative. The concept of the conarrative is crucial for understanding how black Ypsilantians discuss a work ethic in principle and in practice.

MAKING MEANING OF THE CONCEPT OF WORK ETHIC

In documenting how black Ypsilantians articulate their work ethic, this chapter offers a discussion of how they align commitments to certain kinds of work, ideas about "working hard," and assessments of personal motivation. In short, here we compare the normative American opinion to depictions of oneself when actually at work. A critical consideration of what black Ypsilantians reveal about their work ethic helps unravel how they situate themselves in the minimally rewarding and turbulent employment sectors that have circumscribed their lives. It is not a secret that many people often present themselves in a more appealing and socially acceptable manner when asked or expected to define themselves to others (Bryman 2016; Goffman 1959; Harré 1979). However, the nitty-gritty of who these people are becomes more evident when they are asked to talk about specific events or circumstances in their work histories that have to do with demonstrating great effort or investment in their work. Ultimately, conversations that begin with inquiries about one's sense of his or her work ethic but then move into discussing how that ethic was demonstrated in or pertinent to some work experiences allows for insight into how the work ethic is framed in principle and then is argued to materialize in practice. As alluded to by Jerry Jackson, there can be stark differences between the two.

Indeed, the distinction between these two modes of self-expression is critical when the lens is focused on low-income African Americans because of the consistently negative portrayal of them in the public mindset. The very contrasting remarks appearing at the start of this chapter make it tempting to suggest that the *real* Jerry Jackson spoke the second time around. After all, public assessment of lower-income and working-class African Americans often envisions them as uncommitted to putting forth their best effort while at work (Gilens 1999). However, what must be taken into account in considering how these individuals discuss their work ethic, and how it applies to their actual experiences at work, is that nearly all of the people featured in this book acknowledged situations in which they did not uphold their initial depiction of self in terms of a work ethic. Hence, if they initially were lying about how they regarded themselves as workers, why abandon the lie when asked to talk about that ethic as part of their actual work experiences?

We have seen that the work they do is neither glamorous nor highly desirable. It offers little in the way of the kind of material return that they seek and that is necessary to enrich their lives. It also often does little to provide them with a sense of inner pride and value as employees. The work lacks an inherent sense of value. Accordingly, the positive sense of self that is promoted comes from a more abstract notion of what kinds of workers they consider themselves to be. The actual experiences of work facilitate their comments about the shortcomings, problems, and tensions that demonstrate something other than the initial portrait that they present.

The next section of this chapter helps provide more clarity about how people like Jerry Jackson can offer philosophic claims about their work ethic and then explicitly state their limits as far as actual effort is concerned. Separating the work ethic in principle from the work ethic as reportedly practiced captures a more thorough sense of who these people are in terms of what they have done, want or hope to do, need, and expect from the world of work.

THE WORK ETHIC IN PRINCIPLE: EXPRESSING THE FUNCTIONAL SELF

When responding to questions about what it took to find and maintain jobs, all of the black Ypsilantians presented what could be posited as a standard American cultural script of what it takes to get ahead. The qualities that were most often mentioned concerned human capital traits (e.g., possession of a hard work ethic, knowledge of how to work with one's hands, the possession of educational or vocational training credentials) or social capital traits (being connected to people who have secure and rewarding employment, knowing people who seem to know many other people). The importance that people place on each category of traits has been sufficiently documented that the matter requires no elaborate commentary here (see Falcon 1995; Farley, Danziger, and Holzer 2000; Fernandez and Weinberg 1997; Granovetter 1995; Hochschild 1995; Moss and Tilly 2001; Sullivan 1989; Taylor and Sellers 1997; Wilson 1987, 1996). What is especially illuminating is what black Ypsilantians said about the personal qualities required for maintaining work. As they have had some exposure to the world of work, they realized that maintaining a good image in the eyes of managers and other superiors was crucial, and this understanding emerged from their almost always working in highly subordinate places in the world of work.

Nearly every black Ypsilantian identified himself or herself as a hard-working individual. The work ethic in principle boiled down to committing to hard work, timeliness, efficiency, and responsibility. Denise Embers is a 29-year-old high school graduate who attended community college for a short while. Her only form of formal employment was as a parking meter reader. As she put it:

> I figure a job, you know, is a job and I'm here to work. It's like you go to school. It ain't no favorite thing of yours, you know, you might have maybe four, five subjects you don't like but you're there cause you're there and you've got to learn. My work ethic? Do anything to get the job done. That's as plain and simple as work ethic could be. . . . I feel like when I'm there and I'm on the job, I'm on the clock, I'm there to do a service or chore or task, or whatever. Whatever I'm supposed to do, I need to get that job done in that time frame that's allowed because that's what I'm getting paid for doing.

A slew of additional comments reflect the strong similarities in the participants' views:

> I could say basically that I am a very hard worker, you know what I'm saying? I'm good to get along with, you know what I'm saying? Some of the jobs that I had, like I say, I'm a very hard worker—some of the jobs, basically all of them. . . . I messed up myself, you know what I'm

saying? But, I can say, man, a lot of jobs, I've had compliments man, that I'm a good worker. And, I know I'm a good worker, you know what I'm saying, in anything that I do. I know I'm a good worker. It's something that I just mess up on my own, man. It might be drinking or something or something that I do outside of the job, you know what I'm saying, that always affect it. (Larry Lawson, age 35, high school graduate who worked as a parking lot attendant and custodian)

Well, I'm a hard worker. I mean like some days I can come in and just knock my work out, you know. Work all day. . . . I would say I'm a thorough worker. I make sure my work is done. (Greg Garvey, age 24, high school graduate and custodian at the University of Michigan)

Always giving 100%. I just go to work and I just do my best in everything I do. I don't care if it's picking up the trash. I'm gonna make sure I pick up all the trash, not just some of it. I've learnt that from my mom. She always told us, if you gonna do something do it heartily, always. Give it your best shot. Don't half step it. . . . Do it right the first time. Don't have to come back and do it again. (Ann Marie Davis, who has worked in patient care)

I've always been hardworking, honest, always did what I had to do. When people tell me I'm not doing what I'm supposed to be doing and that makes me feel kind of negative because I feel like I always put my best foot forward. . . . I'm dependable. I don't miss that many days only when I'm really sick. You know. . . . Nobody's perfect. There's always something that somebody can improve on. If you want to tell me to improve on something, show me what I need to do to improve on it and I'll try to do better. Like I said, I try to put my best foot forward or try to give you 100%, but nobody's perfect. Everybody could have something that they could do better or more well. (Eric Ellison, a high school graduate who has been a retail clerk and janitor)

Um, I think my work ethic's pretty good though. I'm on time. I'm prompt. I'm doing what I'm supposed to do on the job. I don't like skip over stuff and leave work for another person. Um, I'm accurate. I'm positive. I think I have a good work ethic. (Sabel Janis, who has worked as a temporary clerical)

Nelson Armstrong is a 30-year-old high school graduate who was an office clerk in his only form of formal employment. As he explained:

I have a good work ethic. I listen well, and I do, like maybe a lot of major things that you really say, well, if the supervisor asks you to do that over there, a lot of people will say, "Well, that ain't my job." I'm the type of person that goes ahead to do it, you know. . . . If I do [need any improvements] probably just a little bit. I think probably just work a little bit harder than I have been, just a little bit. But, other than that, I keep a good attitude, so I'm definitely not that—I get along with everybody.

Beth Samuels is a 36-year-old who has worked in fast food. She has graduated from high school and completed some courses in community college. She said, "I'm a people person, I work good around people, I work good with children. I, you know, anything you ask me 9 times out of 10 I can do. You know, you tell me what time to be there, I'll be there. I'm dependable."

Finally, Ralph Remington had the following to say about his work ethic:

Hard worker. Hard worker. Dependable. A good person to work with. I do show up on time. The only time that you won't see me is probably—if you don't see me, then something done happened, you know what I'm saying? I done went to jail or something, or something happened. I ain't the type of person that just don't show up, you know what I'm saying? Like, if I say I'll be there, I'll be there. If I'm not there, something's wrong.

These remarks affirm that Americans place a high value on agency. That is, people like to see themselves as having the capacity to take action on their own behalf. Studies have indicated that those on the bottom rungs of the socioeconomic ladder especially hold to this notion (an overview of such research is found in Hochschild 1995). One of the features of living in disadvantage, this research argues, is that people do not fully submit to the idea that they are wholly powerless to change their personal circumstances. Accordingly, many low-income African Americans in Ypsilanti abide by the creed that they have at least some capacity for action on their own behalf, and they make their case specifically in terms of how they assess their behavior at work. Black Ypsilantians view themselves as fully capable of performing in the world of work. Therefore, even as they struggle to adapt to a changing employment landscape in what is now a postindustrial era and are locked into a vision of a social world that comes with living in the kind of small city that they do, they also strive to imagine themselves as functioning in some way in a future that they struggle to make sense of given their education and work experience deficits.

Many black Ypsilantians said that they are willing to go beyond what is expected of them, and that they are reliable. In talking about their attitudes and dispositions, they exemplified functional selves. That is, regardless of the obstacles and challenges involved in their work situations, most of them described themselves as hardworking, determined, and hopeful rather than despondent or victimized. It should not be overlooked that 87 of the 103 people featured in this book came into this research through their involvement in MichiganWorks!, the job training and information program discussed in chapter 1. Their presence there meant that they were engaged in a tangible effort to try to improve their life situations. Hence, they were perhaps more agentic—more functional—than many other disadvantaged people. However, the great majority of them also attached conditions to their purported work ethic: They will work hard *if* the pay is fair, the job is enjoyable, the work is not demeaning or below their potential, there is accountability, or they feel the need to make immediate provision for a family member. Women were less likely to bring up such conditions but did note that they will not tolerate bad relationships, professional or personal, that hinder them from being a good worker. In fact, many women said they are hardworking because they are independent and have to provide for their children. This is all background to their articulations about being functional selves.

THE WORK ETHIC IN PRACTICE

As almost all of the black Ypsilantians in this book have work histories, they were able to draw upon actual work experiences to supplement their principled claims about their work ethic. The discussion of those work experiences is where visions of how they believe their work ethic emerges in practice come to the surface. Black Ypsilantians did not reject the idea that in order to acquire and keep good jobs one has to work hard, be efficient and timely, be a good colleague, and maintain the proper disposition and demeanor at work. The distinction between black Ypsilantians and those of more privileged backgrounds is that the work experiences of the former positioned them not so much to abandon but rather to modify their principled good work ethic when discussing actual work experiences. Consequently, rather than reject the work ethic in principle, these people consistently expressed a conarrative about a work ethic. This conarrative becomes evident when considering their discussions of how the work ethic is applied to actual work experiences. In considering how and why there was a seeming divergence in discussions of the work ethic in practice in comparison to its framing in principle, it is important to remember the qualities of the work opportunities available to them.

The kind of work that black Ypsilantians engaged in when they did have jobs involved consistent supervision, monitoring, and regulation. It involved punching time clocks, adhering to strict schedules, and coordinating effectively with their fellow workers. Hence, the abilities to get along with others and to deal with supervision in its most literal form were essential parts of the everyday work experience. The inability to escape these demands and expectations also meant that when problems unfolded at work, those occurrences were often tied to these workers whether or not they considered themselves to be at fault for what transpired. Therefore, when the work ethic in principle was not upheld, it was often due to the perception that too much was asked of them given what they were being paid, or that they had to endure some aspect of relations with their coworkers or managers that was unsettling to them.

Much of the discussion assessed in this part of the chapter emerged in response to questions about whether the participant felt that his or her work ethic had ever been challenged. In essence, the nature of the work that low-income black Ypsilanti residents experienced did not inspire them to adhere to the standard American work ethic script. Working in less than desirable jobs for less than desirable pay resulted in less than optimal commitment and performance.

As Vance Ritchie explained when asked if anyone had ever challenged his work ethic on the job, "You're going to get that. I mean, you experience a lot of jobs. That's normal. I mean, I won't get upset about it. I mean, I'll try harder, or you know, that's life."

Others shared similar remarks:

> I learned that I'm a very good worker and I'm very strong minded and that's not always good, because I speak my mind. And, I learned that, you know, you got to watch your managers and supervisors and stuff, because they will try to run over you, you know, and if you don't know the ropes and you don't pay attention to some of the stuff that people

tell you, they will try to get over on you, you know what I mean? (Sherry Lewis)

If I see somebody, you know what I'm saying—if I see somebody that's over me on a job and they're giving me a negative attitude, after a while, I'm going to give them a negative attitude, and I'm not going to give you one immediately because you give me one. I'm going to try to act like I ain't even know nothing. I'm going to act like I don't even know why you acting the way you acting. Once I see that every time you in my presence and you acting a certain way, I'm going to eventually let you know how I feel you acting towards me and we going to have to discuss it and figure it out. (Sam Singleton)

I would describe my work ethic as very positive, um, so into whatever I do, you know, really dedicated to it. Responsible. I take more of a responsibility—that's how I end up with bad jobs, I think, because I take more of a responsibility than I should. You know, like I said, with the higher management, of course they're not going to do the work that I do. I'm going to be busting my tail all day long to get my $10 while you make $20 and you dictating to me how to do it. (Carla Richardson, age 24)

Further making this case, Alice Carlson, who was 28 at the time of the interview, had a few community college courses under her belt, and had been a clerical worker, said:

If somebody wants a job, they got to figure out—first of all, they got to decide, because a lot of people, they just settle for jobs, just because they need a job right now. I mean, when you got bills to pay and you got mouths to feed, you got to do what you got to do, and I understand that, but I'm just saying that, people like me, I don't have mouths to feed. I mean, I'm my whole family. So, I'm not going to settle for a job anymore. I've done that in the past. I don't like it. I don't like that. I'll quit a job and not even tell anybody.

Kennedy Gamble has two kids. She is a 32-year-old office assistant who has completed some community college courses. She said, "I would rather not have a job than work for less than $9.00 an hour. I just feel like it would be a waste of time. And then with the potential that I have, I know that I can do so much, so much. I don't really know if that's right for me to say that, but that's just how I feel."

And Carter Gaston said:

> I would say like, uh, it's probably not going to sound good, but it's
> dependent on something. It's dependent upon me making that good
> money, it's dependent upon me, you know what I'm saying, uh, being
> comfortable in the workplace, that makes everything works out, you
> know. Uh, I've had good work ethic because of reasons like, uh, I
> wanted to, uh, look good for this reason or I wanted to look good for
> that reason, you know what I'm saying?

Carter's job at the time of the interview was in the underground economy. He was fencing clothing. He did this work from the time he was
released from prison until he landed a formal job in retail sales. This job
gave him a sense of responsibility and security that he did not have when
he first got out of prison. It also put him in the position of being sought
after by relatives who needed support, financial and otherwise.

Much like the stories told earlier, Carter had to try to balance work
with the demands and expectations of family, especially his extended
family members. In explaining his approach to work given this condition,
he said:

> But, now, it's dependent upon things. It's dependent upon that pay,
> you know what I'm saying? It's dependent upon those hours being
> flexible. It's dependent upon that location. It's dependent upon things,
> you know what I'm saying, now in my life, you know what I'm saying?
> Now, I don't just do stuff for no reason or for a dumb reason, you know
> what I'm saying? As long as I'm getting what I'm getting, you going to
> get 100% from me, you know what I mean?

Karen Andrews said, "I just speak before I think. And sometimes I say
stuff that I shouldn't say, but it's already out. . . . And I've been in a
situation where I've been arguing with somebody at work. . . . But it's too
late, you know, because for me it's so hard to be humble." Humility was
hard for Karen because, as she explained, the kind of environment that
she was living in mandated that one suppress his or her humility for the
sheer sake of survival:

> I had to tell my son's principal this one time, you know. My son, he
> rough, and he would fight kids and do all types of stuff. And so [the
> principal] said, "Well you know, he shouldn't be doing this and that."
> And I said, "Let me tell you something," I said, "When you grow up in
> an environment like this, if you don't fight your ass is gone." And then
> when you take them to a whole new environment where you supposed

to tell "Not hit, not touch, do this, do the opposite of where you came from." Then you got problems. That's what it is. That's exactly what it is. So, I've always been the one that [says,] "You ain't talking to me and, I don't give a fuck what you say." You know, that's a bit mean. And sometimes, and especially where you got to say wait a minute. You know, sometimes you got to bite your tongue and be humble, and it's so hard.

Mary Dallas, a 27-year-old high school graduate who had worked as an office clerk until she was fired, said:

> I need to work on patience. I need to work on, I wouldn't say kissing anybody's butt, I really, I don't care what they say out there and I don't care what my coworkers say or anybody, I'm not kissing anybody's butt. I feel like you know, that I can respect my employer and he go around me, and they can respect me back. I guess gaining respect would be the thing and then keeping, you know, the respect mutual.

Jesse Harris, a 21-year-old high school graduate and machine operator, said:

> Because I know how to work, I know how to treat people and I know how to deal with situations. The first time, I would take it. I won't say nothing to you the second time you do it. If it's my fault, okay, I understand, but you don't have to be yelling at me. You don't have to be treating me like I'm a little kid, because I'm a man. I'm doing a good job, and doing my job, that's what you're paying me for. . . . So, it's not hard for me, but before I used to tell them, "Get off my back." But, now I learned it's better to talk to people about it, to be humble, to be humble around people, you know, don't take things so personal. It's just a job. Do what you need to do. That's it, basically.

Walter Washington said:

> Teamwork is very [important.] . . . I am actually a loner-type person I've found on my personality, but at the same time, if I'm working with someone or people, I like teamwork because if we do it and get the job done consistently, it'd be a lot easier as opposed to somebody walking, complaining, running on the phone, which they do constantly over here. Just that negative attitude. I know that you don't want to be at work, but keep your mouth shut. Do the job. Go home. . . . Yeah. There's times when I get lackadaisical when I'm frustrated like anybody else. But I always try to do the best I can so I don't want to have to hear anybody else's mouth.

Finally, Ralph Remington said, "I don't like to listen to people some-times. It's all about how you talk to me because if I think you talking to me the wrong kind of way, you know what I'm saying, I'll talk to you in a wrong way, just like I just think you did me, you know what I'm saying? I'll come at you the same way."

In most cases, the work ethic in practice for black Ypsilantians was built on interactions with supervisors, coworkers, customers, and clients in lower-tier service sector work. These interactions sometimes resulted in feelings of assault, threat, or other forms of discomfort. Hence, they gave rise to moments when the work ethic in principle did not hold.

Ann Jimerson, a 34-year-old who processed paperwork at the Univer-sity of Michigan and had taken some community college courses, said:

> I'm that type of person that's just. . . . My supervisor changed from like good to, all right, to, it was just that we bumped heads. We were like, if they could get rid of me tomorrow, they would. That's how I feel. My file is thick. I have been pulled in offices like, "You're not a good team player. Could you try to be a little nicer to your team," but I don't like them. That's what I told 'em. I don't like them. I didn't come here to have to be nice to them or share my personal life with them. I didn't come here to chat.

Another example of the challenge of getting along at work was pro-vided by Sonte Whittles. She is a 27-year-old high school graduate who does patient care and clerical work at a health-care center:

> I do what I need to do and I'm gone. As far as getting along with the supervisors and all that stuff, it could be better. It could be better. I tell them—I don't hold nobody up. I will bite my tongue for oh so long, but I don't hold nobody up. That's probably my biggest issue right there. I get pissed off, and then I leave. I need to learn to control my temper.

She went on to tell a story of conflict that surfaced at work:

> Okay, well they accused me of it, which I actually did do it, but, you know, you couldn't prove it, so get out of here. We went to lunch, but—well, see I came to work early. I came in to work early—this is when I was in a CNA and I got tired of doing the work. And, they wanted us to cut down our nails and stuff. My nails are normally long. My real nails, I have them real long with the, you know, acrylic over them. I don't wear the fake nails. So, they wanted us to cut our nails. I'm like, "I'm not cutting my nails. I'm not cutting nobody, I'm not scratching nobody, my nails is clean. I don't see the problem. You hired me, this is how I was. My hair was done, my nails was done, this is

how I was." "Well, we need you to cut your nails." "No, I'm not cutting my nails. You do not pay for me. You're not supporting me, so you cannot run this outside of the job." So, I had broke a nail or did something, and I went to get it filled at lunch time, and you know, it ran over or was a little bit longer than what it was supposed to be. So, I came back and they was like, "Well, you went to go get your nails done because so and so said this." That's again working with black folk. They were like, "Well, such and such said you went to go get your nails done" and all this other kind of stuff. So, we got to arguing about it and I was like—because my nails were still the same because I hadn't gotten them done yet. I was just waiting and they hadn't gotten to me yet. So, I ended up having to cuss them out and I still had my job, you know. You couldn't prove it. I was outside in my car smoking a cigarette. That's what I told them. "Well, we couldn't find you." "You didn't come outside. I was outside in my car smoking a cigarette."

Almost every black Ypsilantian participant who had ever held a job (which was all but seven of them) reported some moments of conflict or tension at work. Many conflicts were the kinds that caused feelings of minor annoyance. Some resulted in the loss of a job. Almost all took place in work settings where the employees were less than thrilled with the kind of work they did. Low wages guaranteed their persistent disappointment, and uncertainly about the stability of their jobs, their relationship with their colleagues, or their personal situations at home exacerbated those feelings. This is why the work ethic in practice was so conditional.

CONCLUSION

The work environment for these black Ypsilantians usually involved little in the way of creativity and excitement. Instead, work took the form of tedious activities or the kind of highly routinized tasks and responsibilities that typify many kinds of less-skilled, blue-collar employment. Hence, rather than being able to discuss the capacity to be innovative or to think creatively, performance was taken to mean little more than completing instrumental tasks. Part of this meant working with others who had to respond to the same kind of drudgery, yet having to do so while working in concert with each other. The discussion about the work ethic, then, came out of work experiences steeped in talk of task completion. What was noticeably absent in the participants' remarks was any emphasis on creative expression or cognitive stimulation. These latter attributes are more often associated with higher-tier, white-collar professional employment. The world of work for black Ypsilantians rested in the kind of quotidian interactions and encounters that constitute much of the lower-tier labor market. Hence, it is not hard to imagine that states of frustration, if not misery, could emerge from common social interactions at work that overrode workers' attention to work-related production or to service delivery. This is why for many black Ypsilantians the work ethic in practice fell so far short of the standard scripts associated with the work ethic in principle.

SIX
Engaging the Future
Women versus Men

A work ethic is activated by employing a skill set or repository of capabilities relevant to finding work. For this to fully unfold, one must confront, overcome, or minimize perceived and actual obstacles that stand in the way of finding, securing, and thriving in work. This chapter looks at how black Ypsilantians regard their skill sets relevant to employment and how they imagine responding to obstacles and challenges concerning the pursuit and acquisition of good jobs. By linking these two areas of concern, this chapter delivers on what black Ypsilantians believe they possess, need, and must confront or challenge about themselves or their social environment in order to achieve better lives. Much like other issues raised in this book, many of the distinctions fall along the gender divide. More specifically, black Ypsilantians argued that certain kinds of gendered bodies appear more appealing than others, and some more threatening than others, for certain kinds of work.

As made evident previously, the kinds of work that both the men and women identified as best for black male bodies were no longer viable in a postindustrial small city. These bodies were argued to best fit into a type of physical labor that although a hallmark of traditional masculinity also was a hallmark of the bygone industrial era. For the men, then, there was similarity in both what they imagined as good work for themselves and what industrial-era employers regarded as appropriate for them. The work identified as best for women centered on personal care and service provision. Fortunately for them, this type of occupation was much more prevalent in the contemporary world of lower-tier work. Before diving into these critical distinctions, it is necessary to explore the commonalities in what black Ypsilantians claimed to be necessary for finding and maintaining good work.

SKILLS AND ABILITIES FOR FINDING WORK: THE FUNDAMENTALS

What black Ypsilantians articulated as the necessary skills and abilities for accessing and maintaining work is not surprising. These skills consist of what many may regard as common physical, mental, material, and emotional resources. Nearly all respondents agreed that hard work, appropriate presentation of self to employers, and possession of appropriate credentials (especially educational ones) are necessary for obtaining a good job. Moreover, they argued that the kind of work available for themselves requires being attentive and responsive to bosses and managers, as those individuals have extensive control over their fate. Despite some of the difficulties they encountered with such people while at work, they asserted that the seemingly inevitable conflicts, problems, and tensions that arise in the kind of work they are accustomed to doing required that they cultivate some clear and consistent manner of maintaining rapport with management. They also understood that engagement with coworkers was crucial given that the very same conditions applied in dealing with them.

In the participants' minds, a part of the looming image of the factory was that successful work experiences there necessitated teamwork and camaraderie. The kind of individualism that often is associated with white-collar professional employment is not easily imaginable as part of their potential work experience. Hence, a great deal of what they argued about how to best fit into the world of work rested on believing that they had to effectively function with colleagues and coworkers because productive labor in the spheres relevant to them rarely relies on individually oriented work. Hence, collaboration, teamwork, and social relations were acknowledged at least as much as personal productivity.

The following statement by Larry Lawson reflects the sentiments of the great majority of black Ypsilantians featured in this book:

> You got to have communication with your fellow employees. If y'all not getting along, that's going to stir up a commotion somewhere where, you know, it's going to get you in trouble or that person in trouble, you know what I'm saying? That's very important, you know, having communication with your fellow employees, you know.

Along the same lines, Ralph Remington said:

> If you ain't got no good relationship with your boss, you know what I'm saying—it ain't got to be the best but, you know what I'm saying, you don't want like tension. . . . If you and your boss ain't got no good relationship, you know, it could be any time of day that he could just give you the boot, let you go.

He continued:

> [To an employer] a bad person can be anybody off the streets. Have they been convicted of a crime? No. But, you might look at him like, "Hmm, he's on the edge. We'll call you back. . . ." A good person is somebody who comes in dressed all nice, tie, dress pants, slacks, and can talk. If you can talk in conversation with somebody, I think finding a job won't be hard. Like myself? It's not really hard for me to find a job, but sometimes it is. It depends on how you present yourself. That's the main word, present.

Charmain Willis is 21 and has worked as a cashier in retail. She has completed high school as well as some community college courses. She said, "Basically when I get to work, you know, it seems I see everybody start smiling. So that would be always smiling and laughing, and talking to everybody. You know, everybody has . . . make sure everybody has a good time, you know, even though it's work, you've still got to have a good time of work."

Much of the general conversation about the skills relevant to securing jobs focused on how to deal with coworkers, supervisors, and bosses. Many black Ypsilantians placed a significant amount of attention on the degree to which one needed to make a positive impression. This is one example of a broader category of soft skills that matter a great deal to employers (Farley, Danziger, and Holzer 2000; Moss and Tilly 2001). Yet many did not elaborate upon exactly how much these skills matter in comparison to others, or whether there were more or less appropriate times to apply them.

Those who had experienced some postsecondary coursework placed greater emphasis on networks and education. While hard work was equated with better jobs, or at least necessary for good jobs, many also said that communication and self-presentation (in terms of mannerisms, dress, and overall appearance) are also important factors in obtaining a good job. A few respondents argued that it is vital that workers leave their places of employment with good impressions in order to obtain good references. While many respondents credited hard work, presentation, and perseverance as key factors in getting a good job, some also noted that people get good jobs by chance or luck. Across the board, black Ypsilantians argued for the dominant narrative as the basic script for how to access good jobs. Differences emerged when gender surfaced more directly in the conversations.

Only eight black Ypsilantians did not report major gender-related differences in discussing what skills and personal dispositions mattered for approaching future job market prospects (Dante Ellis, Eric Ellison, Oscar Orenthal, Corey Kennedy, Justine Wells, Terri Berrien, Terrance Templeton, and Letisha Combs). Another four reported not being sure if gender mattered in discussing obstacles and barriers for finding work (Tracy Barton, Walter Washington, Ann Jimerson, and Harold Herring). As for the others, gender-specific contrasts began to emerge when they were asked to talk about their personal efforts to adapt to what they saw as the expectations and requirements of the modern world of work. We first turn to what the women had to say.

THE WOMEN

The women had well-articulated short-term plans. They discussed the necessity of knowing oneself, knowing what kind of job one wanted, and whenever possible, not settling for less. The women discussed having appropriate skills and qualifications and maintaining confidence and a positive attitude significantly more than did the men. They also talked about the necessity of knowing what one wants in a job, while men rarely brought this up. Moreover, some women discussed their personality strengths (i.e., being good with people) or skill sets (i.e., the ability to type quickly) as well as their commitment to maintaining confidence and avoiding troublesome people and situations. Essentially, when the women discussed working hard and asserting oneself, self-esteem and confidence permeated their comments. They generally articulated their short-term plans better than did the men, and if they didn't have a plan they discussed the necessity of knowing what kind of job one wants or even asking for help to set goals. In contrast, men tended to be more vague in expressing a workable, short-term goal for gaining or maintaining employment and suggested some unidentifiable force was hindering them from achieving workplace success.

When asked about the chances that African American women have in comparison to men when it comes to acquiring jobs, Kelly Jensen said, "Someone had told me a while ago that, no matter where you work, no matter where you go, the man is going to get paid more than you. That's what they told me. A lady told me this."

Kelly is an outlier among the female black Ypsilantians. Very few of them felt that African American women had fewer opportunities than African American men, and none was as certain about this as was Kelly. This seemingly striking finding becomes more clear when taking into account that despite the challenges facing the women, they were better connected to the lower-tier job markets than were the men. Furthermore, when at work the women encountered others like them—lower-income African American women—doing the same jobs. Few black men were in such a position and almost none were in positions superior to those the women had. Interestingly, Kelly's outlier assertion came not from any work experience (because she had never held a job in her 18 years of life) but from what she said she had heard from friends who did have jobs.

The more common sentiment shared by the women was expressed by Ellen Martin:

> I would say it's easier for a woman to get a job over a black man to get a job. . . . It was like harder for the women back then, you know, than for the men. And now, I would say, women, on the black men, they're open to more job opportunities because the women can work the men's jobs, so the women are getting more and there are more and different things happening than in the last 10 years.

And Sharon Jett, a 20-year-old with some community college experience who worked in retail food, said:

> It's easier for black women than for black men to get a job. For one, because we're women, so they're going to automatically look at that and say, "Well, yeah, we're going to give you this job over this guy." For two, we're a lot more responsible, I think, in a lot of ways than men are. We're more organized, I would say. And, black men, I'd say, are

often very, very, very often stereotyped like in a negative way, as hood-
lums, gang-bangers, drug users, you know.

Finally, Alice Carlson said:

> Black women have an advantage over black men. White men have an
> advantage over black men. If you are an intelligent black woman . . .
> you're going to get yours. . . . Because it's just always like that. I think
> black women have a better chance of getting a job than some white
> men. I don't know. That's the way I see it, because I've never gone for a
> job that I didn't get, because being a minority sometimes can work for
> you.

In comparison to black men, at least, the women generally believed that
they were perceived by supervisors and business owners to be a safer
presence in the workplace. This was so as long as the women did not
engage in stereotypical conduct at work that made them appear to be
unprofessional.

The talk about managers, customers, and clients feeling more comfortable with women was one of several gender distinctions. Another that
surfaced in the women's discussion about skills and resources for fitting
into the world of work pertained to the way in which they talked about
their families as a factor in determining their possibilities. Family talk
centered on how options and interests in work had to be weighed against
meeting the everyday needs of children. As they reported, this posed a
distinct disadvantage for them; the men did not talk in nearly the same
degree of detail about work interests and objectives being compromised
by the everyday needs of their children.

Many of the men in this book are parents. However, only women
consistently discussed work opportunity as contingent upon handling
childcare and other everyday childcare concerns as obstacles to finding
work. In some cases it was because they felt that they would be perceived
as less dedicated to work if they acknowledged their children in the face
of potential employers. In other cases they regarded themselves as liabilities in keeping good work because of the extent to which they focused on
maintaining consistent involvement with their children or because of
their embracing the idea that women with children were stigmatized in
the world of work.

Melissa Higgins, a 27-year-old who did not graduate from high school
and worked in patient care, said, "You know, couple of my friends, just

like me, they got kids. And it's hard. I mean, it really is hard for black women [because of having children] to get jobs, you know."

Alice Carlson said, "Kids just make it so much harder. . . . But when you got children, that's a push, too, because you know you got to do it, because you've got kids to feed."

Mary Dallas said, "[I feel] very insecure [about the job market]. I feel like I have a lot of things going against me. I don't like to tell them that I have kids because then they think there's going to be a lot of problems with that, missed days, no school, whatever, daycare, things like that and if you get a job, you get a woman, you know."

There also was a stark qualitative difference in how women talked about striving for a better future in the world of work in comparison to the men. It is too much to say that a hard line divided the two groups, but it was the case that women tended to fall at the end of a continuum of sentiments ranging from more to less elaborate arguments how future goals would be attained. Women most often had much more detailed plans for engaging the future. Most of the women were mothers with children living with them. Hence, their commitment to such detail may have been due to their conscious sense of work security being necessary not just for themselves, but also for dependents at home who could not support themselves. As such, they offered much more precision about how they planned to move from their current station in life to someplace better. Some examples follow:

> First step is getting some kind of a degree in human services and I plan to do that next year [2001], start my education for my degree. The next step is to continue to dedicate myself to the organization and to make myself available for different things and different programs in the organization. That's about it. That's all I need to do right now. (Jessica Boyd)

> I started volunteering at the daycare and getting to know the supervisor, going in and helping her out, before I even applied for [a job there]. And I prayed a lot for it. I prayed and prayed. Plus I had already went to the school before so they kind of knew me. I graduated from [name of the school] and I was really using that for the betterment of me. [I was] willing to put in a lot of hours without being paid, just so you could give me consideration of getting a job somewhere. (Jenita Yvette)

Well, my future career goal is to go to law school and be an attorney, either with the juvenile court system, or just, I don't know. I'm thinking getting into either law—well, probably law. And, I plan to write a book, do some writing. I just have to enhance my writing skills. My goals—well, those are my goals. To be an attorney. . . . So, my goal is to go to this community college full time, except for this summer—full time until I have enough transferable units to go to U of M and transfer to U of M. I'm in a liberal arts program right now, so just transfer over to U of M, and I'll probably major in either history or poli-sci. So, once I get over there, get my undergrad, and then, I'll probably go in a gradu-ate program, but only a one-year. I don't want to do another two-year program. And then, after that, I'm going to probably brush up on my essay writing, you know, because I want to take the LSAT. So, prob-ably, right after I graduate from U of M, I'm going to take the LSAT, get in a graduate program for a master's, you know, and then just go to law school. (Alice Carlson)

I'm bold, I know what I want first, you know so I think that's the main thing. A person knows what they want. It's not a problem. And like I've said I've always been in the health care field so, it never bothered 'cause there's always been plenty of opportunities for that. . . . Getting that paper work . . . no matter, how much experience you have that paper work makes a difference. A person with experience as well as paper work to go with it. Other than that you can't get a good job. . . . Certain degrees, diplomas, a diploma. Let me start, a diploma, a degree and experience all in line with a degree would make a great job. (Barba-ra Champion)

Finally, Ellen Martin talked about becoming a white-collar professional, which for her implied the kind of employment sector that would gener-ate the level of income that she desired as well as the capacity for person-al control. She said:

Well, right now, I want to go back to school, but I have two kids and, you know, my husband, in the position the way he is right now, my kids, no babysitter, so the only thing I can do is work and go ahead and get my real estate license and daycare license and try to get my own 24-hour daycare so I don't have to worry about nobody watching my kids for me. And then, I'll save up some money and get my own house and rent it out.

Alice Carlson is the only one of the women quoted here who is not a parent. The others have between two and five children and, except for

Ellen Martin (whose husband is unable to work), each is a single parent. Therefore, they make the case for why so much detail was offered by the women. Alice, the outlier here, was once in training to become a flight attendant but discontinued that after becoming pregnant (she later miscarried); she had engaged a higher-tier form of employment than had most of the other women. It is not surprising, then, that given her exposure to relatively higher-end employment sectors, she would offer at least as much detail about pursuing the future as did any of the other women.

Women also talked more frequently about having a good resume, knowing how to be presentable in a job interview, and presenting themselves as professionally inclined and pleasant in the course of job interviews and throughout the job application process:

> I think as long as you have work experience in, as long as your resume looks good, you can get any job you want. I think you can make your resume work for you. That's what I think. I think your resume works any type way you want. (Tracy Barton)

> Listening to people a lot, you know. Where I work now, my desk is right by the front. So everybody that comes in stops at my desk, you know, and talks. Getting along with everybody, you know, even if you don't really care for the person. You know, just treating them fair, you know. (Samantha Jermain, age 34)

> A lot of jobs they don't want to hire you if you like have a gap in your employment history. 'Cause say like if I worked a job for three months, I try not to put that one on my employment application [because] they'd be like "Well, you didn't work in the last six months and blah blah blah," and you had to think of something to say. . . . [You have to be] a reliable person, a person an employer can see that is willing and probably able to do the job, a person with good verbal skills, a person that, you know, not really penmanship [but] a person that can fill out an application without making misspelled words and stuff like that cause they look at that, and a person who can answer the questions. You know how they have like a survey of questions at the end, a person who can answer those to the best of their ability without lying and stuff, just a positive person. (Alaina Tannenbaum, age 32)

> Interpersonal skills, talking on the telephone, I'm really good at that. I don't know if that was from all those clerical jobs. And I'm at a customer service position recently, so those telephone skills help with that

position, being able to talk to people and being able to greet people. So I know that I'm a people person. I just learned it from really all my jobs. Dental assistant, because I have to greet the patients and seat them and, just, you know, conversate with people. I like to get into seeing how people feel and try to—I'm one of those save the world people. I know that I can't do that, but for a long time I wanted to save the world so I would just always be in like, how you doing? And just always into people. I like to see people happy. (Kennedy Gamble)

Make sure you have a resume, good references. Make sure you, you know, have an open mind. That will get you anywhere. Make sure you have good conversation, boy. Good conversation will get you a lot of things. It might not feel like it, but you'll get far with good conversation. (Sherry Lewis)

The level of detail provided by the women reflected their ability to be much closer to developing a plan for engaging good jobs, rather than just maintaining a hope of doing so or a fixation on the limits standing in the way of doing so. Even the men perceived black women as being more elaborate and detailed when it came to discussing future prospects for work.

Black Men Discussing Black Women

Turning to what the men had to say about the potential for black women to fit into the modern world of work sheds further light on the distinctive situation of the women. Much like the women, only a few men felt that black women have fewer employment opportunities than did men.

Nick Barnes is 23 years old and did not complete high school. At the time he was interviewed he was unemployed, although he did report doing some day laboring in construction. He has one child and lives alone. He said:

I think today it's the females that are going to get all the most good jobs. This is like a female world, now. Females starting to get more dominant and things. Males, we starting to slack off, now. I don't know what it is, but we starting to slack off. These females out here doing them.

Anton Mintz, a 26-year-old, said:

I used to be like girls are just smarter than boys. . . . But it's not that . . . because see like boys, you know, men, we got this damn thing, like this ego thing, you know what I'm saying, that keep us from a lot of stuff. You know, women, more like, okay, no matter what, you all always find a way with it, you know what I'm saying?

Brent Hobson, age 32, argued that black women have an advantage because of the combined effects of their race and gender status:

You have a greater number of black women going to college, and pursuing advanced degrees, than black males. And so to a company who's looking to diversity their staff, you know, would seek a black woman, or a minority woman because it fulfills two needs. . . . It fulfills the need for women, and it fulfills the need for minorities.

Sam Singleton also asserted that women have an advantage:

I mean, everybody know that women got a way of doing a lot of stuff. I ain't saying like [matters that pertain to] sexual harassment and black males or whatever. I'm just saying when a woman walks in, they going to make their presence felt. They going to dress decent. I ain't going to say all women, either. . . . I'm just saying women. I can't really get in too deep about how they dress and all that.

As evidence for his opinion, Sam said, "I think it's majority women who work here [in the MichiganWorks! office], you know what I'm saying? And, they all dressed up, looking nice, taking care of business."

Montel Mason also argued that black women were better off than he was:

'Cause I feel like with the different laws out here, that when hire, when you look at a black man, you're hiring a black man. You're hiring a minority, ok. With affirmative action, I don't know if it still exists, you fulfilling that quota. But, when you hire a black woman, you fulfilling two quotas, 'cause you're hiring a woman and you're hiring a minority, so basically you're knocking out two birds with one stone. . . . So I think it's more easy for them to get a job.

And Nelson Armstrong said, "It seems like women can get more out of life and get more help than a man can. . . . You know how they say, 'It's a man's world'? I think it's a woman's world. But, it just seems like they give in to the women more. . . . And it seems like some women will give another woman a job before she gives it to a man." According to him, sexism worked to women's advantage. "And men, sometimes, they don't look at a woman as just being a woman, they look at her for different reasons, you know, 'I'll give you this job if we can do such and such and go out or something.' It just seems like a whole lot of things work out for women."

Finally, Carter Gaston said:

> I know what it's all about, man. I mean, like, uh, the white man is trying to survive, man, and he know the only way he going to survive, man, is he treat our woman good because that's the only way he going to—like, he treat the black woman better than he treat his own woman. He prostitute his own woman. He put his own woman on Hollywood Boulevard. He make millions and millions and billions and billions of dollars on his own woman off pornography, right? You know what I'm saying? Man, don't get me wrong. We got some black women that do it, too [but] he solicit his own woman, but he treat the black woman like a queen, don't he? Yes, he do.

Underlying conspiracy theories and traditionally sexist portraits of women were clear indicators that the men thought black women were better positioned for the modern world of work. The women's commentary about themselves offered much more precise interpretations about why this appeared to be the case. That they could be so much more precise is further evidence that both male and female black Ypsilantians regarded black women as better positioned (at least in terms of knowledge of practical things to do and steps to take) for work in the future. As we will see, the men were much more focused on challenges and obstacles perceived to be standing in the way of a more secure future and much less on creating a vision of tangible possibilities for that future.

THE MEN

Research conducted since the 1990s has demonstrated the difficulties that African American men face in trying to secure employment. During this time, researchers uncovered the extent to which being an African American male is a detriment to finding and securing good employment (Pager 2007). Accordingly, the general distaste that employers have for black men has been well documented (Farley, Danziger, and Holzer 2000; Freeman 1992; Holzer 1996; Holzer, Edelman, and Offner 2006; Kirschenman and Neckerman 1991; Moss and Tilly 2001). This literature has explored how employers maneuver in order to reduce their prospects of hiring African American men, especially if the job involves significant interface with customers or clients. More specifically, this research has uncovered how much African American men are regarded as a liability for interfacing between customers or clients and the retail businesses and agencies that are providing services. The social implications of being an African American male in contemporary labor markets were not missed by the residents of Ypsilanti, as both men and women spoke extensively about how much one had to work to portray images that contrasted with anything that employers could associate with low-income African American male identity.

The attention given by black Ypsilantians to the pitfalls for black men in regard to the labor market was extensive. When they were asked to talk about obstacles and barriers to finding good work, a great majority of the discussion focused on the perceived problems faced by black men, what they need to do to confront these problems, and for the women, how they took pleasure in not having to do so (some exceptions to the prevailing point of view that black men have it worse are discussed later). Upon being asked, virtually every man commented that the barriers and obstacles that African American men faced made their situation more problematic than that of African American women.

A sampling of the views of some of the men follows:

> It's a woman's world man, now, you know. The women starting to have more opportunities than the males is having in 2001. . . . It's like, a couple of years ago, I was with my friend, and he was trying to go fill out a job application and they was like, "We ain't hiring no more males. We only hiring females now." So, I'm like, okay. It's a female game, now. (Nick Barnes, 23, day laborer who did not finish high school)

> I see all kinds of jobs for, uh, office work, you know, clerical or secretarial, or even call center, customer service, or even maybe doing some mortgage work in an office setting, closing, you know, things like that. And, uh, the way that I see it, you know what I'm saying, is if women could just learn those skills as far as, uh, the office skills, you know what I'm saying, I think there could be a lot more jobs available for them. But, even if a man learns skills like that, the jobs wouldn't be, you know, readily available for him, you see what I'm saying? Because, I think when they look for somebody to do office work, they look for a female. I think there are more jobs available in an office setting than there are any type of setting. I mean, there are some jobs like construction work, you know, you're not looking for women to do construction work. But, there are more jobs available in an office setting than there

are in construction. (Kent Paulson, 27, who attended some community college and worked in fast food and was fired from a job at Ford Motors)

Grant Hilton is 31 and has a GED. He has been a short-order cook but has been fired twice from that work. He has much of the same feelings about the women's advantages as does Montel Mason. He said that he often helped his girlfriend prepare her resume and material for job opportunities that he believed could never come his way because he is a man. He explained:

> She can get a job as a secretary making good money right now. Uh, a black man is not going to be in that position, especially if he's any size. If you are any size right now, white men are totally intimidated, right up front. They don't even want to—especially dark-skinned. You just wrong. But, for a woman, she can work her way around that.

In wrapping up his discussion of the detriments of being a black man in search of work, Hilton said:

> [White employers are] afraid—I have no clue [why]. That's something I would like to know. They don't understand that we are just people and we have to live just like they do, you know. I have no idea what they're afraid of. Maybe they're afraid for their jobs. Maybe they're afraid that they're really going to see you do your job.

Many of the preceding comments reflect how black men are trying to come to terms with a confusing and not fully accessible postindustrial world of work and the possibilities for them to fit into it. Grant Hilton presented an almost stereotypical portrait of the (female) secretary situated in an office setting. He implied that this setting was no place for a black man. Grant's remarks and those made by the others attest to a contemporary world of work in which black women appear to these men to have more presence and more agency than might have been the case in the past. The men maintained that office work was more fitting for women. In holding to this belief, they demonstrated much about why they were disconnected to the major sites of postindustrial labor while remaining beholden to the industrial sphere, even as it had become more elusive to them.

In expressing another kind of sentiment from the men's perspective, Ralph Remington discussed how the government designs its policies to favor women, thus placing black men at an inherent disadvantage when it comes to trying to improve one's life situation:

> I believe that they want the black men to work, and you know, they want the black women to just, you know, sit on back, you know what I'm saying, and, do nothing. Why you think they put them government checks out there for them to get, you know what I'm saying? They got them where they got them feeling like, you know, they don't got to work, you know what I'm saying? "Okay, I got a man who do work a job, who make good money." And then, you know what I'm saying, she might have like four or five different niggers, you know what I'm saying? As long as she got that check, got that nice little lump of money coming in, you know, can't nobody tell her shit, you know what I'm saying? She going to go get her outfit instead of paying her light bill, you know what I'm saying? Get her nails done instead of buying her kids some shoes, you know?

Many men talked about needing to have the right personality as a way to convey that there's some unidentifiable thing they lack that is required for good jobs. For men, the talk about searching for a good job seemed to strip a lot of their sense of self away, while engaging in such talk did not have that kind of effect on the women. Recall the words of Nick and Nelson in the previous section. While talking about black women, both indicated that black men were not moving ahead, but neither could offer any precise reasons why. Accordingly, these and other men insinuated that some social force—the economy, white Americans, legal processes, or the maintenance of a threatening personality type—was what was working against them.

While women have some shorter-term, concrete goals in mind or say that they need help executing a better game plan, men talk about their bigger dreams or are not willing to say they need help devising a more concrete game plan. Men talk about wanting to have a house, a car, provide for kids, "get recognized," or start their own business, while women don't bring up these bigger achievements. Men also appeared to be much less sure about what is inhibiting them from being reliable and dependable. The women, in short, were more focused on plans while the men were more focused on goals.

Only 20 of the men mentioned education as important in order to get a good job. Only 14 of them mentioned needing to possess the appropriate character traits, such as having a positive attitude, working hard, and personality. While women were more likely to talk about professionalism in creating resumes and conducting oneself during interview processes, men emphasized being assertive and having a likeable personality in order to win employers over. Their focus on likeable personalities invokes their sense of what employers refer to as soft skills, yet for these men, the utilization of soft skills takes on a particular salience because such efforts not only can convey to employers how these men may manage interactions with colleagues, clients, and customers in a work site, but also how that effort can help overcome the pernicious public portrait that such men believe they bear in the minds of many white Americans.

Another dimension of how black men perceived their public identities to be so blighted surfaced in their talk about legal processes as among their biggest obstacles. These included having to submit to drug tests and abide by child support laws, operating without possessing a valid ID, and possessing a criminal record. Closely associated with the last points of emphasis was the men's greater preoccupation with staying out of trouble in order to maintain a job, and they did so to a greater degree than emphasizing what it took to become "accepted" in a workplace.

Corey Kennedy, age 22, did not complete high school. When he did find work it was uniformly restricted to the fast-food industry. He said, "It's hard, especially with people that got felonies. They ain't—like a person like me, they ain't really trying to give me any job, like a real good job, unless I have somebody to help me out to get a job."

For the men in particular, possession of a prison record was commonly referred to as a source of employment problems. Grant Hilton said:

> If you have a record, almost none [chances of getting a job]. I mean, because you got to realize this is a very competitive world, and they're looking for anything to say that you're not capable to have this job. So, they can just as soon hire somebody with better criteria. So, it's a lot of situations out there where black people have to step up to get their own. . . . If you got a felony, you'll never get a job. I'm trying to move out the country now, believe it or not. . . . It's that tight. We were talking about trying to get out of the country because of the laws that they're setting up for us is ridiculous. . . . I mean, you might as well say, nowadays, if you're black, you're going to jail. Ain't no way around it. It's some way that you're going to go to jail. That's horrifying. I mean, I got kids I'm trying to take care of. I can't afford to go to jail for some petty things.

The problems that African American men in particular encounter with the criminal justice system are well documented (Alexander 2010; Mauer

1996). Like many black men throughout the country, those in this analysis who had experienced incarceration or had been convicted of a crime maintained that meaningful work was even farther beyond their grasp than might be the case for other men. As James Jencks, a 38-year-old whose primary work experience was as a custodian, stated:

> That's another problem . . . about being a felon and been in prison before . . . 'cause most jobs, they exclude you if you have felonies, and so do companies. They don't care what it was [that resulted in one's conviction]. You know . . . you're excluded immediately. . . . Everybody was talking about UPS [as a good job]. UPS is a company that won't hire you if you have a felony.

Finally, Ralph Remington, who had attended community college and worked as a custodian, put it this way:

> Once they get out of incarceration and you fill out that application form and they read it and look it over and that one main part, it gets them — have you been convicted of a crime? Once they check that, yes, they're going to ask you, "What have you been convicted for?" "Oh, I murdered three people." They're not going to hire nobody like that.

Although the men mentioned the necessity of working hard (in a physical sense) and being on time, they were more inclined than the women to discuss their approach to work in a conditional way. That is, they were more likely than the women to assert that they would work hard when the job was good. They argued that they were willing to be hard working *if* the pay were good, *if* it were a job they enjoyed, *if* it were not cleaning toilets, *if* they were not going through a lazy spell, *if* there were supervision, and, with less emphasis and elaboration than the women, *if* they had a family to care for. Most important, the men appeared to be imprisoned by expectations such as concerns about wage earning rather than assertive about what they could do in the world of work.

Much was said by black men about what they must do to minimize, if not eliminate, the social deficit created by being a black male. In fact, both the men and the women expressed a range of ideas and opinions on the matter. Such conversation provided another opportunity to take stock of what it meant for low-income African Americans in Ypsilanti to live in an environment that allowed them significant access to white Americans and some degree of exposure to the mainstream worlds of work. That is, rather than explicate in abstract what black men needed to do to circumvent the detrimental status of being black and male in the world of work, many spoke in highly specific and concrete terms. Ultimately, exposure to the world of work, even if only tangentially, taught many of the low-income African Americans of Ypsilanti not only that black men suffered particular disadvantages in finding work, but also that success in finding and keeping good jobs was predicated, at least in part, on ensuring that one does not appear to promote or reflect any of the attributes associated with what is commonly understood to be urban black masculinity. Put in more simple terms, the common point of emphasis here was the need for black Americans to be mindful of how much they had to manage themselves in public so that they did not appear to be the kind of African American that sociologist Elijah Anderson (1999) described as "street."

In his assessment of the behavior and expressiveness of urban-based black Americans, Anderson (1999) argued that certain African Americans exhibit a threatening public demeanor. This depiction is a part of Anderson's larger framing of certain urban-based, low-income African Americans as "street" people, as the kinds of people who portray the image that many Americans find to be threatening or intimidating. This manner of public expression and agency is contrasted with that of "decent" people, which Anderson explains to be those African Americans who reflect what many might regard as more normative (read more consistent with middle-class white American) characteristics.[1] In order to secure good jobs, then, the black men expressed the need to displace themselves from the public identity of being street, and both men and women spoke about how much more challenging it was for men to do so in the eyes of potential employers.

As Nelson Armstrong explained:

> Being a black man these days, you got to take a lot. A lot of us have to take a lot to get a lot, or to get anywhere and anything out of life. You might have a person over there that don't like you just because of your race or whatever, and then they might not really care for the black woman that much either, but it's a woman, too, so—man, I just really think as a black man, we have the worst in the world. . . . So, therefore, like a lot of black men that's ignorant—and, I'm not saying by school or anything, just act ignorant, it ain't cool. It's not good, especially when we're already being looked at a certain way. Go ahead and do something positive.

Garvin Smalls, a 27-year-old machine operator with some community college experience, talked about how he felt confident about potential employers whom he talked to on the phone, but things changed once he met with them in person. As he explained, "You know, long hair, guy's got braids, they figure you're a thug. . . . And me having the braids don't help, so I'm about to cut these things."

Ronald Gregory said, "They walk around in their clothes singing, when they looking for a job. They got a baseball cap on sideways, applying for a job. Then they get in the place, they're going to talk that thug talk, you know."

What this meant for low-income black male Ypsilantians is that they were keenly aware of the importance of presenting themselves in ways that did not reflect what they understood to be the stereotypical negative image of black masculinity. The men spoke of the need to be careful about how they wore their hair, how they dressed, what language they used, and how they interacted as contexts wherein they could be viewed as fitting into the negative imagery. In discussing how African Americans from Ypsilanti tend to approach work prospects, nearly half of the residents made mention of being loud, flashy, and thuggish, and how that influences job opportunities. Men were especially sensitive about how their body size might operate to limit their employment prospects.

The Benefits of Being a Black Male

Much of the discussion about the detriments of being black and male had to do with the perceived intimidation that black male bodies presented to potential employees and coworkers. A couple of the men, however, discussed the detriments associated with what some perceive to be imposing black male bodies as an asset for securing work.

Jackson Jerls, a 21-year-old who did not finish high school, at one point had worked for a delivery service. He said:

> It might be more opportunities for a black man, you know, especially if he's willing to do more physical labor. You know, you can get a job working construction or something like that, labor or something like that. And, that's some decent money, but you really earn it. . . . Right now is building season, but when it's winter, you'll get laid off. But, you can find those types of jobs, laborers and whatnot. There aren't that many out there right now, but you can find a job.

More tellingly, Mark Niles had served in the military, where he had worked in security and begun developing a sense of how his body offered him an advantage for working as a bodyguard once he completed his service. He said:

> People felt safe around me. I made them feel safe. I started doing body-
> guard work. And I started guarding people, executive protection, mon-
> etary bank drops and stuff like that. . . . Using my size and my color
> was an advantage because if you've got a big black guy protecting you,
> other black guys, they won't bother you. . . . And that was the mentality
> of people that I was around. . . . You know, they would even say this . . .
> you know, "this my big bodyguard here." So they thought they were in
> charge because I was [their] bodyguard, but in order for them to stay
> alive and stay safe, they have to do what I said, and I feel good about
> that, because I was in control and I knew what I was doing.

Mark etched out a vision of control, utility, and purpose even though one can imagine that as an employee, he was still at the beck and call of those for whom he worked. Even in his telling of a moment of success at work (he had only served as a bodyguard near the end of his military service, and for the past several years had worked only as a custodian and day laborer), he drew upon the same preference for manual work that so many other male black Ypsilantians regarded as the best kind of work for people like themselves to do. Aside from these comments and a few others, black men did not report having much of an advantage in the contemporary world of work.

Black Women Discussing Black Men

Cherry Robards was quite deliberate in expressing her views on the challenges of black men finding employment. She said:

> I think it's harder for black men to get good jobs. I think it's particularly
> harder for African American men that are dark-skinned African
> American men. And, if you're big and dark-skinned I think it's really
> particularly hard for you to get a good job, because it's true people do
> seem to be intimidated.

In discussing the prospects of black men in work, Alice Carlson said, "You got to be really overqualified for your job when you're going up against somebody in corporate America who's white when you're a black man, because they'd rather give it to a black woman before they give it to you." Alice, like many others, explained that black women appear to be less threatening and can make themselves appear to be more appealing to white male bosses.

Aletha Mack, a high school graduate who worked as a nurse's aide, said:

> I know being a black woman you would get hired a lot faster than a black man because I mean just look. If you go outside on the corner what do you see? You see black males standing around, pants hanging off their tail. They're not doing anything because they've been stuck with this mentality that all the White man doesn't want, I can't do that. It's negative thinking. And you can't stay around negative thinking, you're going to think negative therefore you're going to be negative.

The very kind of social service work that seemed appealing and potentially accessible to black women was regarded by several of these women as a risky prospect for black men. In making an argument that was consistent with what some other women thought, Pauline Hamilton, who did not complete high school and whose work history largely rested in retail customer service, said:

> I don't think a man, like, would go to an office setting, unless they were characterized as gay, because I know this one man, and he works at the Social Service board at the food stamp office, and—because, you know, he has little curls, this and that, and they characterize him as gay. I've only met him a couple of times, but, you know, people are like, "Yeah, he's gay. He works in the office." Whereas, if you seen a white man doing that, they wouldn't say that, anyway, to me. I don't think so, because they're supposed to be more, um, white collar anyway. So, it differentiates between the color. And, you see a lot of black men working in harder jobs, I think . . . like factory jobs, services, because they have that lack of education.

The vision of black men as victims of malaise and misfortune was not lost on many of the women. Carlese Randle, a 34-year-old high school graduate who had worked as a grocery store clerk until she became pregnant, supported this perspective:

> It's hard. Well, black men, especially for black men. All they really do is sell drugs, hang out on the streets, and that's no place to be for them. They need to have some positive thing in their life and motivation. You know, just seems like they don't want to do any work. Yeah, as a black person, this is really different. I know it's not my problem, but as a black person, it is awful to see my people like this.

Alice Carlson said:

Black men are more dominant than white men, you know, their expression, how they are, they're just strong. They're just more, you know, — and, white men, I don't know, they're intimidated by black men, you know, especially somebody on their level. They're used to a black man being beneath them economically, and then here's somebody who has an education just like you, um, you know, everything that you have and can compete with you, and then there's somebody on a higher level that can make a decision about "Oh, I can give this black man a chance, or am I going to give this white man a chance," and they'd rather give the white man a chance, because they don't want to give the black man a chance because black men have always been—they want to keep them on that level where they are not, you know, they can't compete. They don't want to—they want a black man to prove that they're inferior to them, almost. Kind of like that.

For several women, however, men were perceived as being at an advantage for the more traditional (yet no longer accessible) kinds of work opportunities in Ypsilanti that harkened back to the days of the large factory. Alaina Tannenbaum has worked on an assembly line in food services. She said:

Uh, men could . . . with . . . with a high school education or GED could probably get a better paying job than a black woman because, you know, men can go out there and work. They can use they strength like, you know, concrete, drywall, paint, things like that. They can make good money doing that without even having an education. So, yeah, they probably would.

Melissa Higgins said

Oh, well, I mean, you know, men, they got, they all . . . It seem like they all . . . they always get the upper hand. I mean, like they get the good jobs in the plants, but they, so-called they strong or whatever. But I'm strong too, shit. You know. Like . . . a mechanic's job, a woman can do it too, but they'll hire that man before they'll hire that woman.

Sherry Lewis said:

Men have a more better chance of getting a job with benefits because they look for more like factory work, construction work, you know, manly jobs. Us women, we look for jobs that aren't going to kill us, you know, by the time we're 40, you know what I'm saying? So, it's like, you know, I don't know. I really couldn't say from a man's point of view, because I have never—I've worked in factories, but I didn't last long, you know what I'm saying?

Finally, Lori Watson said:

> Yeah [black men have an advantage over black women]. If it has to do
> with lifting or you know, just construction jobs, but a lot of times wom-
> en don't want to do those jobs anyway . . . because I think if a woman
> went in for a job um dealing with construction, I don't know if she
> would get the job because if another guy, a black guy came in and
> wanted the same job, I think they would hire him before her.

In black women's discussion of the advantages that they believed
black men had for finding good work, the image of the factory endured.
Unfortunately there was not much else that they identified as advanta-
geous for these men in the pursuit of the good jobs. Most women saw the
men as stuck in place, either by their own accord, external forces working
against them, or a combination of the two.

CONCLUSION

Despite the litany of problems raised about the struggle to fit into the
world of work, none of the black Ypsilantians in this book sounded com-
pletely despondent. They did not surrender to being complete victims of
their circumstances. Many sounded as if they had developed tough skin
and had fought throughout their adulthoods to maintain confidence and
hope. Indeed, the eight individuals who had experienced incarceration
expressed a greater emotional preparation for engaging in that struggle.
However difficult the world of work might be, it was not as difficult as
was the world of incarceration. Many black Ypsilantians discussed their
opinions as if they were living through unique and highly personal experiences, but on the whole they were actually conveying quite similar
sentiments.

However, while both men and women recognized the importance of
education and professionalism while at work, it appeared as if the wom-
en were prepared to fully embrace these qualities, while men were more
inclined to discuss these qualities as absences in their lives that ultimately
strip them of their sense of a stronger self. For example, the men reported
being angry that they have to shave their hair or conscientiously manage
their bodily comportment to get a job. The women certainly recognized,
but almost never complained about, having to change their appearance in
order to engage the workforce.

NOTE

1. There has been some degree of controversy over Anderson's framing of "street" versus "decent" African Americans, resulting from the terms being used to make analytical distinctions about particular kinds of people in a hardened and rigidly applied manner. As scholars such as Sudhir Venkatesh (2000, 2006), Mary Pattillo (1999, 2007), and I (Young 2004) have argued, some urban dwellers may appear to be street in some aspects of their public interaction and comportment while decent in various others, and this holds for African American urbanites other than the gang member or substance abuser. While Anderson does indicate that people can move across and between these framings, he often applies them in a comprehensive manner to the people in his studies, which disavows a vision of them as inherently decent in any capacity.

Conclusion

Place and Possibility for Small-City Black Americans

Twenty years have passed since I started fieldwork in Ypsilanti. Since that time, I have never left the city, and Ypsilanti has never left me. I remain a customer and client of several businesses in Ypsilanti, and I set foot there almost weekly. In the decade since I stopped doing formal fieldwork there, I have continued to think about how unique this small city is for understanding the experiences of African Americans concerning work and work opportunity. Looking back, I remain intrigued by what has been steadfast about that city over time. Black Ypsilantians still yearn for better jobs and better life situations. Despite their hopes and dreams, the manufacturing sector has not returned. The changing nature of work opportunity in Michigan makes it clear that it will not.

A symbol of such irreversible change is the vacant Visteon plant just north of Interstate 94. Weeds grow in the cement cracks of its parking lot. Located directly across the street from the northern end of that lot is a hall that once housed the plant employees' union headquarters. (Visteon's employees constituted their own United Auto Workers local.) The union local, which secured the fringe benefits and services that made work in that factory so rewarding, is gone. The building is now an evangelical church. As for the plant, in 2018 a property-for-sale sign appeared on its grounds. That sign, conveying how what used to be a place of vibrant activity is no longer, is visible to anyone traveling on I-94 headed west toward Ann Arbor or east toward Detroit.

The Ford Motor Company's Willow Run plant, located immediately east of Ypsilanti, was a five-million-square-foot facility that had 40,000 employees during its mid-twentieth-century peak. In recent decades it has declined as well, beginning prior to my fieldwork. In 2010 its most recent owner, General Motors, closed the plant as part of its bankruptcy protection effort. As that plant maintained a larger physical structure than Visteon's, its vacancy provides a much more ominous image of industrial decline for the region.

161

Despite these developments, Ypsilanti underwent a bit of a revival in the second decade of the twentieth century. Efforts were put forth to rejuvenate the downtown district. Several new businesses, including restaurants and small shops, popped up on or near Michigan Avenue. Several also emerged in Depot Town, the historic district that is about half a mile north of the Michigan Avenue downtown area. These venues cater to a largely white American clientele. African Americans and other people of color also frequent these establishments.

Rammos barbershop, my introduction to Ypsilanti, is now a few blocks north of the location where I first encountered it. Today the owner is the only provider of services. Instead of gregarious conversation engaged in by a group of men, the chatter now takes place between customers and Marty, the owner. High-volume exchange occurs only when several customers are present at the same time. Otherwise, one can have a casual conversation with Marty that requires neither the demonstrative expression nor the social bantering that is commonplace in barbershops that serve African Americans. The fried chicken take-out shop just east of the former Visteon plant has changed ownership several times throughout the years. Having not actually visited the business in several years, I know this only from driving by and taking note of the storefront awnings and signage that have come and gone.

Public housing in Ypsilanti also has changed a bit in recent years. Renovations and upgrades have occurred. Paradise Manor has been refurbished and is now Sauk Trail Pointe Houses. The public housing units on Harriet Street (near the southwestern edge of Ypsilanti) have been renovated. New single-family dwellings have been built. The one major change that has not occurred in the city is the creation of a revitalized employment sector for black Ypsilantians. Hence, the circumstances and conditions that undergird the research resulting in this book remain in play. Save for what is now a more extended period of industrial decline, the story told here about Ypsilanti over a decade ago is very much the story of Ypsilanti today.

The core challenge addressed in this book was why one should think about the small city when considering the plight of African Americans. In addressing that question, *From the Edge of the Ghetto* has offered a unique case study of regionalism. The book puts forth a testimonial about how small-city conditions impinged upon the lives of African Americans. In doing so, it illustrates how even if their imaginations of future possibilities in the world of work were similar to those shared by large-city-based, low-income African Americans, the work experiences that gave rise to those imaginations were highly circumscribed by the small-city geography encapsulating their lives.

The preceding pages have elucidated the ways in which connections among race, space, and employment function in a small city. Black Ypsilantians were not embedded in an expansive blighted community, but rather in a blighted condition in a town on the periphery of a more affluent small city. Accordingly, the more prolific images of widespread crime, disorder, and decay that often surface in studies of the African American poor are offset here by the emphasis on how opportunity was imagined to be located elsewhere rather than squarely within an identifiable downtown sector. Their visions of opportunity were affected by a diminished industrial sphere rather than by the emergent postindustrial domain located next door.

Work opportunity was linked to a sphere of employment in Ypsilanti that, when it existed some time ago, was rewarding. This is evident from the private housing that once grounded a more economically secure black community in Ypsilanti. In the past, black Ypsilantians could take advantage of opportunities afforded by the industrial order. Today, the proliferation of technology has benefited people in other places while facilitating confusion and concern for black Ypsilantians.

Like other low-income African Americans, black Ypsilantians desired not simply work opportunities, but employment prospects that would allow them to achieve some stability in the workplace, the chance to develop and apply some meaningful skills on the job, and the chance to move up in the workplace through promotion and the acquisition of greater responsibility (Young 2004, 2006). That disadvantaged African Americans held to such desires is not startling. What is surprising is the extent to which gender divides appeared as these interests were further defined.

The men especially desired work that would afford them a strong sense of self-respect and at least some positive social acknowledgment. They wanted benefits that would compensate for injuries resulting in an inability to work. The women desired work opportunities that would allow them to commit to family needs and interests, especially given the often turbulent situations of families experiencing economic constraints.

Essentially, they believed that a good job is one that stabilizes family life by paying enough money, by accommodating family time, and by offering enough flexibility to allow people to handle family crises and effectively provide for their children.

The gender divide was crucial in extrapolating how people think about where they are in today's world of work and where they expect to be in the immediate future. Black Ypsilantians experienced hardship and all struggled to make sense of the world of work absent the factory and without the kind of work that a factory presence directly supports in a small city. Yet for the women, the struggle was made easier by an ability to transfer the kind of work that they were invested in into visions of meaningful future opportunities. In many cases, that meant thinking about how to transfer informal childcare, domestic service opportunities, food preparation, and other such informal and lower-tier work into imagined careers in the service sector. More important, the women were also much clearer about the necessary steps to take in order to try to improve their prospects.

It makes sense that the men often seemed much more imprisoned by the very model of good work represented by the factory in twentieth-century, small-city America. After all, in past decades the factory had been a core site for work opportunities for men more than women. More concerning was that these men were also imprisoned by having a less-detailed imagination of how to move forward. In part this was because these men were fit to serve in the twentieth-century industrial era. They identified meaningful work as that which allowed them to construct and create in the most material of ways. Even if they recognized the threats that came with such work—injuries on the job and bodily fatigue—this kind of work made sense to them because it involved putting their bodies into creating a tangible, material product. Such work also provided them with consistent wages and the benefits that could do for them and their families what wages alone could not. They desired to be recognized and affirmed as competent and capable individuals at a time when their own perceived skill sets—an ability to build, construct, and do the kind of work that seems like what men should do—are less immediately translatable to future work opportunities. This was compounded by their seeing black women move beyond them in the world of work. Accordingly, many of the men had great difficulty imagining what to do to catch up. In fact, both the men and the women had difficulty imagining how the men could catch up.

In comparison to the men, the women were considerably more focused on taking incremental steps that could help them find their way in the social service sector. They also were motivated to provide for their children. When thinking about work, this compelled them to focus on meeting the immediate needs of family members and not so much on what kinds of work would suit them best as individuals. It was not the case that the men failed to think about family. However, they often did so by way of thinking that what was best for themselves would also allow them to serve their children and families. The women were more inclined to argue about interests for the future while putting others (mostly their children) more directly into their line of focus.

The men struggled to get beyond the notions of work directly associated with the industrial sphere. They were less sure about what to do to get ahead and more sure about the circumstances and conditions working against them. Consequently, they remained in deep wonder about what could possibly work for them in the short-term future. They fully accepted that their bodies were liabilities in the modern world of work (and the women indicated that they felt the same way about black men). The men believed that absent a conscious effort to minimize or circumvent feelings of threat and anxiety on the part of potential employers and coworkers, their very bodies put them in a deficit position in the modern world of work.

Aside from the strong gender distinctions, much of what I learned from Ypsilanti's struggling African American residents resulted from my deep reflection on the ways in which I served as a character in my own study. I am an African American who was born and raised in New York City. As a resident of a large city that makes a huge footprint on contemporary notions of the urban-based African American experience, I came to regard myself as something of a foil throughout the period of research and reflection on the fieldwork and data. My initial expectations, vision, and perspective contrasted with those of black Ypsilantians, and my awareness of the contrasts drove my thinking about what was going on for them. Thus, the analysis appearing here was built from my consistent consideration of difference.

Most significantly, I learned to rethink my orientation to space, especially as it has been construed in a large city such as New York. In my
imagination, the physical space where good jobs exist has always been
downtown. For black Ypsilantians, good kinds of jobs were not bounded
by a business district or in the downtown area. Rather, they were imagined to be in places not easily definable or locatable. I also learned much
about the effects of living in a community where the good job throughout
recent history was construed by residents either to be one type of job or in
strong reaction against that kind of job. Even if black Ypsilantians did not
actually experience work in automobile manufacturing, it became pivotal
for talking about work opportunity because someone in the family history had experienced a good job there or had had particularly bad experiences working in that sector.

I also learned to rethink why people who reside in proximity to what
many might consider to be a better place could also perceive that place to
be so distant and uninviting. No longer would I think that proximity
could be a proxy for familiarity and the comfort that often comes with it.
As a child living in the East Harlem section of New York City, a mere city
street divided my residential community from a more privileged section
of Manhattan called Yorkville. While growing up in the 1970s and 1980s I
knew which side of the street was home and which belonged to other
people. Yet when I was a child, Manhattan—where East Harlem is located along with New York City's central business districts and a great deal
of the city's prosperity—never struck me as wholly foreign. Most of the
other parts of Manhattan were wealthier and whiter, but for me they also
were at least reasonably familiar and accessible.[1]

Ann Arbor, my current home, is closer in physical proximity to Ypsilanti than much of Midtown Manhattan (as the business district is commonly referred to in New York City) is to my community of East Harlem.
Yet for many black Ypsilantians, Ann Arbor was both different and
foreign. Therefore, I came to experience how difference and unfamiliarity
were rooted not exclusively or necessarily in geographic distance but
rather in the divergent histories and fortunes of these communities. Realizing this led me to embrace a new perspective on the ways that place
operated in the lives of African Americans. The historic presence of
African Americans in large cities allows for overgeneralizing about how
they think about place in relation to work-related opportunity and possibility. Rather than thinking about the large city as a template for black

Americans, the Ypsilanti case actually reveals how the large-city context constitutes its own type of regionalism.

My reflections also have led me to consider how I have been both connected to the Ypsilanti experience for lower-income African Americans and an outsider as well. That is, I have shared institutional and social spaces with such people but have never lived among them. Accordingly, my situation resonates with some of the leading African American sociologists who have conducted studies of communities in which they reside or that they regularly frequent in their nonprofessional lives. Sociologists such as Elijah Anderson and Mary Pattillo have conducted several studies in communities in which they reside (Anderson 1990, 1999, 2011; Pattillo 1999, 2007). Some of their key arguments address concerns and circumstances that were a part of their lives prior to committing to researching them.

In the case of Elijah Anderson, a large part of his research interests involves the ways in which residents negotiate public interactions in disadvantaged neighborhoods or in the public spaces bordering those neighborhoods and more privileged ones. Ultimately, in his work Anderson effectively illustrates how some of the interactive practices that he studies and interprets are the very ones that he has employed in his own social negotiations of his neighborhood. For Mary Pattillo, a key point of her analysis is a social tension that she recognized prior to doing fieldwork. That tension resulted from relations between her neighbors of more privileged socioeconomic class standing and those of a lesser class standing. In the work of both sociologists, readers are invited to consider much about the authors' self-reported behavior in the field. The authors also come to understand how that behavior models some ways to resolve some of the social problems their work was intended to address.[2] As a nonresident of Ypsilanti, but someone who entered the city with personal objectives prior to forming a research agenda, I did not perform a study of my neighbors as much as of people with whom I had previously sought to find commonality and with whom I also found stark differences. Hence, the contribution made by this work emerges from realizing what I did not know very well about my field site rather than what I understood at its onset.

My evolving imagination of how African Americans in Ypsilanti thought about and were affected by place enriched my capacity to envision how their imagination functioned as a muscle for them. In this case, that muscle was constrained. The ways in which place situated their imaginative muscle demonstrate how a small city can leave a huge impact on how people think, especially when they are prevented from thinking in certain ways about the future (even as such thinking unfolds for people living a short distance away from them). Imagination as a constrained muscle, then, leaves people stuck in place—and here I refer to place as a physical property—not only because of limited material opportunities such as lower-quality jobs, but also because of what living amid them does to limit the capacity to conceive of alternatives. I caution that this point must be delivered with great care, because it may seem that the solution for black Ypsilantians is simply to dream bigger and better. Arguing that they must do so does no justice to the conditions that they face. Instead, specific kinds of interventions are necessary to promote more effective, future-focused thinking on their behalf.

First, it must be understood that imagination is triggered by real-world experiences. Therefore, any prospect for adults to dream bigger and better must take into account how much their personal histories of struggle result in looking toward the past in order to imagine a better future. This being the case, there remain some lingering questions for those sensitive to the plight of black Ypsilantians and folks whose lives are similar to theirs. What might become of small-city African Americans? What might become of people who live in a context where looking backward is often all some of them can do to figure out how to make a better future? What steps can be taken to help them move forward while they remain in a place that seems to keep them stuck in time?

In answering these questions, it must also be noted that black Ypsilantians do have something in common with the large-city poor. Like the men I studied in Chicago (Young 2004) and Detroit (Young 2006), the low-income residents of Ypsilanti face nearly insurmountable obstacles and pressures in trying to make ends meet in their small city that has seen better days nearly half a century ago. The men and women in this book have not found themselves in stable work environments. They have struggled with finding and maintaining jobs that deliver to them the monetary returns that they feel are sufficient for meeting their personal and familial needs. In essence, they face the concerns, pressures, and anxieties that confront larger-city low-income African Americans. However, in thinking about possibilities for a better future, one point of strong difference between Ypsilanti and the big city remains.

Unfortunately, Ypsilanti is not the kind of city that will get bailed out through massive external attention and delivery of resources. As was the case in its more prosperous past, economic developments in the broader geographic region will make the biggest difference for the city itself. Yet those developments must connect with the very kinds of people who inhabit Ypsilanti. Researchers and economic developers forecast that the state of Michigan has experienced a recent decline in its goods-producing industries and manufacturing, and Detroit has continued to experience losses in jobs and wages over the past decade, especially in jobs involving low-education goods production and low-education service provision (Glazer and Grimes 2015).[3]

Other analysts claim that the areas of growth in the next decade for the state include energy, food and agriculture, water technology, transportation, health, and information technology (Austin, Good, and Kolluri 2017). Small city that it is, Ypsilanti need not attain great job growth in any of these sectors in order for black Ypsilantians to experience significant growth in work opportunity. For a city of roughly 30,000 residents, small growth (the arrival of a single plant or industry) can make a huge difference. However, whatever may transpire as massive growth for Michigan, and particularly its southeastern region, will likely circumscribe the particular opportunities for growth in that city. More important, these developments will also create critical context for what black Ypsilantians must learn about employment opportunities in the future as well as how to best position themselves for them. This all speaks to the need for them to learn to better imagine how new sectors of employment may become relevant for them and to acquire the training and certification to enable access to these sectors.

The radical step in addressing the plight of black Ypsilantians, then, is to invest in reeducation. Job training and job placement centers, including centers such as MichiganWorks!, are understandably already burdened with the task of simply trying to fit people into jobs for the mere sake of their own institutional survival. Yet these centers may be the only possible sites to offer black Ypsilantians a renewed education about the modern world of work in a postindustrial age. For example, black Ypsilantians need a better understanding of what an emerging green economy might mean for work and work opportunity going forward. Although running the risk of forcing them to think about the kinds of work their immediate ancestors did, which motivated their parents and grandparents to escape the South, this kind of education might also allow them to better grasp how they can both survive and endure the changed landscape of work opportunity in their region.

In the very short term, what male black Ypsilantians in particular need is access to opportunities that enable them to rethink and adjust from the historically embraced idea that physical capabilities can meet the needs of the modern world of work. The green economy and other agribusiness developments might be the very space for people who continue to maintain that going to work with their hands and bodies is the best kind of work for them.

Finally, the threatening public image of African American males, which according to black Ypsilantians appears as much in the small city as it does in big-city America, must be eradicated. This can be done through a balanced blend of such men's willingness to manage if not avoid behaviors that reflect that threat and employers and business owners committing to changing their outlooks on these men. Neither of these tasks is an easy project, yet the latter must happen if any change in the employment prospects of these men is to occur. If it can transpire, this kind of transformation ultimately may enable pockets of opportunity to unfold for these men in the social service delivery arenas that women are already so thoroughly focused on.

As for the women, even though they can imagine a more clear path toward employment stability, they also experience the burden of childcare demands and concerns—and the reality of being vulnerable in the world of work because of the children that are or might one day be in their lives—at levels that far exceed family-based threats for the men.[4] All of this is to say that the fate of black Ypsilantians, and struggling African Americans more generally, is not fully in their own hands. The rest of us have work to do so that healthy working communities can emerge that inevitably will benefit us all.

NOTES

1. I readily admit that my situation contrasted with those of many of my peers in East Harlem. For most of my childhood I was educated in Catholic schools located in some of the wealthiest parishes in New York City. I was also in the unusual situation of being a child in a white-collar professional family that, due to my parents' political orientation, resided in one of the most socioeconomically disadvantaged communities in New York City. Hence, the point I make here only concerns my changing under-

standings of how people envision, react to, and encounter public space. While I recall that many of my peers seemed to maintain the same outlook as I did toward the rest of Manhattan, this may not have been the case for others who lacked the material resources and mobility options afforded to me.

2. I explore more fully the ways in which these and other ethnographers serve as objects in their own analysis in Young (2013).

3. Between 2010 and 2014, jobs declined by 8.9 percent in low-education goods production by 14.4 percent in high-education goods production, by 1.0 percent in low-education service production, and by 3.4 percent in high-education service production (Glazer and Grimes 2015).

4. A litany of research has documented the challenges that women face in the world of work precisely because the possibility of pregnancy or the actuality of having children causes them to be perceived as less reliable workers (Correll and Benard 2007; Glynn 2014; Moen 1992; Parker 2015; Perry-Jenkins 2005; Pew Research Center 2015; Raley, Mattingly, and Bianchi 2006; Sandberg 2013; Sayer 2005; Slaughter 2016; Smock and Noonan 2005; Wang, Parker, and Taylor 2013; Williams 1999, 2010).

Appendix

Portrait of the Research Participants

Name	Gender	Age	Education	Employment	Family Status	Crime/Record
Karen Andrews	F	25	Some college/ community	Aid, machine operator, fast-food work	Three children & boyfriend at home	N/A
Lena Antonio	F	25	Some college/ community	Office clerk	One-year-old daughter, lives with father	N/A
Nelson Armstrong	M	30	HS graduate	Unemployed, some office clerk work	Six children, married to the mother (separated)	N/A
Dominic Banks	M	24	GED & some college	Unemployed (selling drugs), retail clerk, fast food ($10/hr)	One child, lives with girlfriend	N/A
Robert Barber	M	19	HS graduate	Barber ($400/wk), physical plant ($8/hr)	One child	N/A
Nick Barnes	M	23	Some HS	Unemployed, construction ($125/wk)	One child, lives alone	N/A
Cathy Barnswell	F	21	HS graduate	Nurse aide ($10/hr)	Three children, not married	N/A
Tracy Barton	F	25	Some college/ community	Student services at University of Michigan ($300/ wk), aide, patient care, office work ($9/hr)	Two children	N/A
Lisa Battles	F	18	Some HS	Housekeeping	No children	N/A
Martin Bensen	M	24	GED	Truck loading ($8.50/hr), manual work, unemployed	One child, not married, lives with mother	Previously incarcerated
Geri Benton	F	28	Some college/ community	Unemployed, food service	Three children	N/A
Terri Berrien	F	24	Some college/ community	Admin. asst. for temp agency/unemployed	Pregnant with first child	N/A

Name	Gender	Age	Education	Employment	Family Status	Crime/Record
Brock Bevins	M	37	Some college/community	Temporary laborer, stock clerk	No children, no wife	Previously incarcerated
Brandy Bollins	F	36	Some HS	Unemployed, cashier ($8/hr)	Two children, separated	N/A
Jessica Boyd	F	43	?	Receptionist/bank teller, quit a job due to racism	Three children, divorced	N/A
Jayne Butcher	F	36	Some college/community	Patient care ($12/hr)	Two children, not married	N/A
Alice Carlson	F	28	Some college/community	Clerical at WA Community College ($600/month), flight attendant, mail sorting (laid off last job)	No children, not married	N/A
Barbara Champion	F	39	Some college/community	Unemployed, aide, patient care ($10.50/hr)	Four children, separated	N/A
Darryl Collison	M	32	Some college/community	Domestic/house care ($9/hr)	Five children, lives with uncle (?) & girlfriend	N/A
Letisha Combs	F	31	Some HS	Unemployed, store clerk, van driver for program ($8/hr)	Five children, not married	N/A
Anita Cullen	F	27	HS graduate	Flight attendant (did not pass probation period), cashier, office clerk ($19/hr)	Married, no children	N/A
Ted Cummings	M	20	Some college/community	Short-order restaurant host ($8/hr), maintenance crew ($18/hr)	Lives at home with parents, no children	N/A
Mary Dallas	F	27	HS graduate	Unemployed, office clerk (fired from last job) ($10/hr)	Three children, lives with boyfriend	N/A

Name	Gender	Age	Education	Employment	Family Status	Crime/Record
Lanice Daniels	F	39	HS graduate	Patient care ($7.50/hr)	Four children, divorced	N/A
Rick Darnett	M	30	HS graduate	Unemployed, teacher aide in Detroit public schools (fired) ($14/hr), store clerk ($8/hr)	Two children, lives with them & their mother	N/A
Ann Marie Davis	F	31	Some college/ community	Patient care ($9/hr), aide, patient care, newspaper delivery	Five children	N/A
Carly Earls	F	25	Some college/ community	Childcare center ($8/hr)	No children, not married	N/A
Dante Ellis	M	28	Some college/ community	Car painter ($400/wk), car painting, short-order cook	No children, lives with parents	N/A
Eric Ellison	M	31	HS graduate	Janitor at public schools ($8/ hr), grocery clerk, custodian	No children, lives with girlfriend	N/A
Denise Embers	F	29	Some college/ community	Parking meter reader ($18/ hr), cashier, office clerk	One child	N/A
Desire Forman	F	31	Some college/ community	Hospital customer service ($10/hr), file clerk, small business receptionist ($8/hr)	Three children, married	N/A
Brian Fuller	M	26	GED	Temp in physical plant (City of Ypsilanti) ($10/hr)	Two children, lives with girlfriend & children	Previously incarcerated
Carl Fulton	M	41	Some college/ community	Maintenance	Two children & wife	N/A
Kennedy Gamble	F	32	Some college/ community	Dentist office assistant ($12/ hr), aide, customer service ($9/hr)	Two children, not married	N/A

Name	Gender	Age	Education	Employment	Family Status	Crime/Record
Greg Garvey	M	24	Some college/ community	Custodian ($11/hr)	Lives with girlfriend, expecting first child	N/A
Carter Gaston	M	28	Some college/ community	Unemployed, aide, office clerk ($15/hr)	Two children & wife	Previously incarcerated
Loretta Gentry	F	31	Some college/ community	Unemployed, aide, data entry ($8/hr)	Three children, married	N/A
Carmen Granderson	F	22	Some college/ community	Unemployed, aide, airline agent (left due to pregnancy, which failed), cashier ($9/hr)	No children, no spouse	N/A
Timothy Green	M	21	GED	Factory machine operator ($8/hr), package delivery ($8/ hr)	No children, lives with girlfriend	N/A
Ronald Gregory	M	35	Some college/ community	Unemployed, welding, maintenance ($9/hr)	One child, divorced, lives with girlfriend	N/A
Pauline Hamilton	F	21	Some college/ community	Unemployed, customer service	No children, no spouse	N/A
Jesse Harris	M	21	HS graduate	Unemployed, machine operator, fast food ($9/hr)	No children, lives with girlfriend & her son	N/A
Harold Herring	M	36	Some college/ community	Fast food ($8/hr), mail sorting	No children, no spouse, lives with parents	N/A
Melissa Higgins	F	27	Some HS	Unemployed, aide, patient care ($7/hr)	Five children, not married, lives with children & her mother	Previously incarcerated

Name	Gender	Age	Education	Employment	Family Status	Crime/Record
Grant Hilton	M	31	GED	Unemployed, short-order cook ($11/hr), fired twice from such jobs	Seven children, not married, lives with mother of two children	N/A
Brent Hobson	M	32	Some college/community	Unemployed, fast food ($8/hr, quit)	No children, no spouse, lives with parents	N/A
Henry Hollister	M	32	Some HS	Unemployed, aide, roofing, per diem construction ($8/hr)	One child	N/A
Jerry Jackson	M	42	HS graduate	Unemployed, General Motors	No children, separated	N/A
Desmond James	M	19	Some HS	Unemployed, none	One child, lives alone	N/A
Corinne Jamison	F	24	Some HS	Unemployed, childcare, store clerk ($400/wk)	No children, not married, lives with mother & her boyfriend & siblings	N/A
Sabel Janis	F	31	Some college/community	Unemployed, clerical, temp ($9/hr)	Three children, lives with boyfriend	N/A
James Jencks	M	38	HS graduate	Temp agency, clerical ($7.50/hr), janitorial ($11/hr)	Two children, separated	N/A
Edward Jenkins	M	38	Some college/community—disability	No work due to disability	Four children, married (2nd time)	N/A
Kelly Jensen	F	18	Some HS	Unemployed	One child	N/A
Geoff Jerguson	M	32	Some HS	Unemployed, maintenance ($8/hr, fired)	One child, not married, lives alone	N/A
Jackson Jeris	M	21	Some college/community	Delivery service ($7.50/hr), store clerk ($12/hr)	One child, lives with his mother	N/A

Name	Gender	Age	Education	Employment	Family Status	Crime/Record
Samantha Jermain	F	34	Some college/community	Steel inspector ($12/hr), motel housekeeper ($15/hr)	Three children, divorced	N/A
Reese Jersey	M	21	Some college/community	Construction, personal service ($12/hr for both)	One child, lives with roommate	N/A
Sharon Jett	F	20	Some college/community	Cashier, food retail ($7.30/hr)	No children, lives with mother & other relatives	N/A
Ann Jimerson	F	34	Some college/community	Clerical at University of Michigan ($11/hr), aide	Five children, separated	N/A
Corey Kennedy	M	22	Some HS	Unemployed, fast food ($5/hr)	One child, not married, lives with mother	Previously incarcerated
Larry Lawson	M	35	HS graduate	Unemployed, custodial, garage attendant ($8/hr, fired)	Three children, not married	N/A
Sherry Lewis	F	24	Some HS	Unemployed, University of Michigan custodian ($8.75/hr)	One child, not married, lives with boyfriend	N/A
Aletha Mack	F	39	HS graduate	Unemployed, nurse's aide ($11/hr)	Four children, not married	N/A
Ellen Martin	F	23	HS graduate	Unemployed, receptionist, food preparer ($7.75/hr), laid off from K-Mart	Two children, married	N/A
Trent Martinez	M	25	GED	Unemployed, auto detail shop ($200/wk)	One child, lives with girlfriend	N/A
Montel Mason	M	21	Some college/community	Unemployed	One child, lives with girlfriend	N/A

Name	Gender	Age	Education	Employment	Family Status	Crime/Record
Anton Mintz	M	26	GED & some college	Unemployed, tire changer at auto store ($7/hr)	Three children, lives with girlfriend & two children	N/A
Marvin Morris	M	29	Some college/community	US Navy, patient care, store clerk ($7/hr)	Three children, not married	N/A
Mark Niles	M	37	Some college/community	Custodial, maintenance, repair for Ypsilanti Public Housing ($10/hr), aide	Four children, divorced, lives with girlfriend	N/A
Lonette Odell	F	33	Some HS	Unemployed, van driver ($7/hr)	Five children	N/A
Lana Odett	F	30	Some college/community	Customer service at a store ($190/wk), aide, patient care	Two children	N/A
Oscar Orenthal	M	22	HS graduate	McDonald's ($7/hr), movie theater usher	Two children, lives with mother & relatives	N/A
Kent Paulson	M	27	Some college/community	Unemployed, Ford ($23/hr, fired), fast food	No children	N/A
Elena Perry	F	22	Some HS	Store clerk ($7/hr), housekeeping ($100/wk)	Two children, lives with boyfriend	N/A
Carlton Pitts	M	24	Some HS	Unemployed, on public aid, never worked	No children, lives with brother	N/A
Alfred Ramsey	M	36	Some HS	Unemployed, aide, partner at car dealership ($320/wk, fired)	No children, homeless, stays with friend	Previously incarcerated
Carlese Randle	F	34	HS graduate	Unemployed, aide, grocery clerk ($4.25/hr, left due to pregnancy)	Three children, lives with children & her own mother	N/A

Name	Gender	Age	Education	Employment	Family Status	Crime/Record
Richard Ranson	M	32	HS graduate	Unemployed, short-order cook ($9/hr)	Three children, lives with children & girlfriend	N/A
Tonisha Rawls	F	37	Some college/community	Unemployed, custodial services ($14/hr), light labor, office work ($10/hr)	Two children, lives with them & boyfriend	N/A
Jermain Redd	M	36	HS graduate	Unemployed, odd jobs, aide, lawn care, car oil changer ($9/hr)	Four children, lives with girlfriend & two children	N/A
Ralph Remington	M	21	Some college/community	Custodian ($200/wk)	No children	N/A
Carla Richardson	F	24	Some college/community	Unemployed (laid off from fast food, $17/hr), clerical, cashier for car parts store ($8/hr)	One child	N/A
Vance Ritchie	M	23	HS graduate	Unemployed, UM Hospital ($6.25/hr, fired after being arrested)	No children, not married, lives with aunt	Previously incarcerated
Cherry Robards	F	34	Some college/community	Unemployed, aide, clean linen UM hospital ($12/hr, quit)	Two children, divorced	N/A
Darma Rodden	F	33	Some college, 2 assoc. degrees	Unemployed—disability, grocery cashier ($8.25/hr, fired)	No children, no spouse, lives with aunt	N/A
Destiny Russell	F	27	HS graduate	K-Mart clerk ($8/hr), cashier ($6/hr)	Two children	N/A

Name	Gender	Age	Education	Employment	Family Status	Crime/Record
Beth Samuels	F	36	Some college/community	McDonald's ($7/hr, quit over sexual harassment), carpet maker ($8.50/hr, fired)	No children, lives with boyfriend	N/A
Carlton Simmons	M	35	HS graduate	Unemployed, store clerk ($10/hr)	One child, lives with girlfriend & her four children	N/A
Sam Singleton	M	21	Some HS	Unemployed, aide	No children, lives with girlfriend	N/A
Garvin Smalls	M	27	Some college/community	Unemployed, machine operator ($8.25/hr)	One child	N/A
Alaina Tannenbaum	F	32	HS graduate	Assembly line ($8.50/hr), aide, food service, assembly line ($8/hr)	Two children	Previously incarcerated
Terrance Templeton	M	22	HS graduate	Patient care (fired), unemployed, food preparer ($9/hr)	No children	N/A
Penny Walton	F	32	Some HS	Unemployed, aide, store clerk ($18/hr, laid off)	Three children	N/A
Walter Washington	M	32	GED	Machine operator ($9/hr), bus driver, machine operator ($9/hr)	Two children, married	N/A
Lori Watson	F	20	HS graduate	Unemployed (left job to have child), clerical for a garage hospital ($7.50/hr)	One child	N/A

Name	Gender	Age	Education	Employment	Family Status	Crime/Record
Justine Wells	F	24	Some college/community	University of Michigan custodial service ($10/hr), aide, assembly ($8.50/hr)	Pregnant with first child, single	N/A
Linda Wells	F	28	HS graduate	Unemployed, aide, fast food ($7.75/hr)	Three children, married	N/A
Carlotta Weston	F	29	HS graduate	Clerical ($7.25/hr), aide, ($7/hr, fired)	Three children, roamed (?) lives with two of her children	N/A
Sonte Whittles	F	27	HS graduate	Unemployed, aide, clerical, patient care ($9/hr)	Four children	N/A
Nancy Wilmington	F	27	Some college/community	Unemployed (at-home mother), aide, receptionist, clerical ($9/hr)	Four children, married	N/A
Charmaine Willis	F	21	Some college/community	Retail store work ($8/hr), cashier ($6.25/hr)	No children, not married, lives with mother & siblings	N/A
Jenita Yvette	F	27	Some college/community	Childcare, aide, store security, housecleaning service ($10/hr)	Five children	N/A

References

Acker, J. 1990. "Hierarchies, Jobs, Bodies: A Theory of Gendered Organizations." *Gender and Society* 4: 139–158.

Ackers, George Karl. 2014. "Rethinking Deindustrialisation and Male Career Crisis." *British Journal of Guidance & Counselling* 42, no. 5: 500–510.

Adler, William M. 1995. *Land of Opportunity: One Family's Quest for the American Dream in the Age of Crack*. New York: Atlantic Monthly.

Alexander, Michelle. 2010. *The New Jim Crow: Mass Incarceration in the Age of Colorblindness*. New York: The New Press.

American Fact Finder. 2010. "United States Population." https://factfinder.census.gov/faces/nav/jsf/pages/community_facts.xhtml.

Anderson, Elijah. 1990. *Streetwise: Race, Class, and Change in an Urban Community*. Chicago: University of Chicago Press.

Anderson, Elijah. 1999. *Code of the Street: Decency, Violence, and the Moral Life of the Inner City*. New York: W.W. Norton.

Anderson, Elijah. 2011. *The Cosmopolitan Canopy: Race and Civility in Everyday Life*. New York: W. W. Norton.

AreaConnect. 2006. "Crime Rate Comparison Ypsilanti vs. Ann Arbor." http://ypsilanti.areaconnect.com/crime/compare.htm?c1=Ypsilanti&s1=MI&c2=ann+arbor&s2=MI.

Austin, John, John Good, and Akaash Kolluri. 2017. "Jobs, Michigan & Leadership in the Economy of Tomorrow." Michigan Economic Center report.

Barnes, Sandra. 2005. *The Cost of Being Poor: A Comparative Study of Life in Poor Urban Neighborhoods in Gary, Indiana*. New York: State University Press of New York.

Baron, Ava. 2006. "Masculinity, the Embodied Male Worker, and the Historian's Gaze." *International Labor and Working-Class History* 69, no. 1: 143–160.

Bartlett, Donald L., and James B. Steele. 2012. *The Betrayal of the American Dream*. Philadelphia: Public Affairs.

Bates, Beth Tompkins. 2012. *The Making of Black Detroit in the Age of Henry Ford*. Chapel Hill: University of North Carolina Press.

Bergmann, Luke. 2008. *Getting Ghost: Two Young Lives and the Struggle for the Soul of an American City*. Ann Arbor: University of Michigan Press.

Binelli, Mark. 2012. *Detroit City Is the Place to Be: The Afterlife of an American Metropolis*. New York: Metropolitan Books.

Boyd, Herb. 2017. *Black Detroit: A People's History of Self-Determination*. New York: Amistad.

Bryman, Alan. 2016. *Social Research Methods*. Oxford: Oxford University Press.

Budd, John W. 2011. *The Thought of Work*. Ithaca, NY: ILR Press.

Burkitt, Ian. 2008. *Social Selves: Theories of Self and Society*. 2nd ed. London: Sage Publications.

Callero, Peter L. 2003. "The Sociology of the Self." *Annual Review of Sociology* 29, no. 1: 115–133.

Carr, Lowell J., and James Edison Stermer. 1952. *Willow Run (Work, Its Rewards and Discontents): A Study of Industrialization and Cultural Inadequacy.* New York: Harper & Brothers.

Cayton, Horace, and St. Claire Drake. 1993 [1945]. *Black Metropolis: A Study of Negro Life in a Northern City.* Chicago: University of Chicago Press.

Churchwell, Sarah. 2018. *Behold America: A History of "America First" and the "American Dream."* New York: Bloomsbury.

City-data.com. n.d.-a "Crime Rate in Detroit, Michigan (MI)." http://www.city-data.com/crime/crime-Detroit-Michigan.html.

City-data.com. n.d.-b "Ypsilanti, Michigan." http://www.city-data.com/city/Ypsilanti-Michigan.html.

Clum, Kimberly A. 2008. "The Shadows of Immobility: Low-Wage Work, Single Mothers' Lives and Workplace Culture." PhD dissertation/thesis, University of Michigan, Ann Arbor.

Coleman, James S. 1988. "Social Capital in the Creation of Human Capital." *American Journal of Sociology* 94 (supp.): S95–S120.

Collinson, David A. 1992. *Managing the Shopfloor: Subjectivity, Masculinity and Workplace Culture.* New York: Walter de Gruyter.

Correll, Shelley J., and Stephen Benard. 2007. "Getting a Job: Is There a Motherhood Penalty?" *American Journal of Sociology* 112, no. 5: 1297–1339.

Crowley, M. 2013. "Gender, the Labor Process and Dignity at Work." *Social Forces* 91, no. 4: 1209–1238.

Dolgon, Corey. 1994. "Innovators and Gravediggers: Capital Restructuring and Class Formation in Ann Arbor, Michigan, 1945–1994." PhD dissertation/thesis, University of Michigan, Ann Arbor.

Dudley, Kathryn. 1994. *The End of the Line: Lost Jobs, New Lives in Postindustrial America.* Chicago: University of Chicago Press.

Editorial Board. 2012. "'America's War Zone': Our View; Crime and Corruption at Crisis Levels in East St. Louis." *St. Louis Post-Dispatch* (Missouri), May 6, A16.

Falcon, Luis M. 1995. "Social Networks and Employment for Latinos, Blacks, and Whites." *New England Journal of Public Policy* 11: 17–28.

Farley, Reynolds, Sheldon Danziger, and Harry Holzer. 2000. *Detroit Divided.* New York: Russell Sage Foundation.

Farley, Reynolds, Howard Schuman, Suzanne Bianchi, Diane Colasanto, and Shirley Hatchett. 1978. "'Chocolate City, Vanilla Suburbs': Will the Trend toward Racially Separate Communities Continue?" *Social Science Research* 7, no. 4: 319–344.

Feagin, Joe R., and Melvin P. Sikes. 1994. *Living with Racism: The Black Middle-Class Experience.* Boston: Beacon Press.

Fernandez, Roberto M., and Nancy Weinberg. 1997. "Sifting and Sorting: Personal Contacts and Hiring in a Retail Bank." *American Sociological Review* 62: 883–902.

Freeman, Richard. 1992. "How Much Has De-Unionisation Contributed to the Rise in Male Earnings Inequality?" In *Uneven Tides*, edited by Sheldon Danziger and Peter Gottschalk, ch. 4. New York: Sage.

Gauen, Pat. 2012. "Hanging on to Hope in East St. Louis: Motivated Outsiders, Insiders Keep Working Together Despite the Discouragement of Persistent Violence." *St. Louis Post-Dispatch* (Missouri), September 27, A17.

Gergen, Kenneth. 2000. *The Saturated Self: Dilemmas of Identity in Contemporary Life.* New York: Basic Books.

Giddens, Anthony. 1991. *Modernity and Self-Identity: Self and Society in the Late Modern Age.* Stanford, CA: Stanford University Press.

Gilens, Martin. 1999. *Why Americans Hate Welfare: Race, Media, and the Politics of Anti-Poverty Policy.* Chicago: University of Chicago Press.

Gillette, Howard. 2005. *Camden after the Fall: Decline and Renewal in a Post-Industrial City.* Philadelphia: University of Pennsylvania Press.

Gini, Al. 2001. *My Job, My Self: Work and the Creation of the Modern Individual.* New York: Routledge.

Glazer, Lou, and Don Grimes. 2015. "Michigan's Transition to a Knowledge-Based Economy 2007–2014." Institute for Research on Labor, Employment and the Economy, University of Michigan, Michigan Future Inc.

Glynn, Sarah Jane. 2014. *Breadwinning Mothers, Then and Now.* Washington, DC: Center for American Progress. http://cdn.americanprogress.org/wp-content/uploads/2014/06/Glynn-Breadwinners-report-FINAL.pdf.

Goffman, Erving. 1959. *The Presentation of Self in Everyday Life.* New York: Doubleday.

Granovetter, Mark. 1995. Getting a Job: A Study of Contacts and Careers. 2nd ed. (with a new preface and a new chapter updating research and theory since the 1974 edition). Chicago: University of Chicago Press.

Grossman, James R. 1991. *Land of Hope: Chicago, Black Southerners, and the Great Migration.* Chicago: University of Chicago Press.

Hamer, Jennifer. 2001. *Abandoned in the Heartland: Work, Family, and Living in East St. Louis.* Berkeley: University of California Press.

Harrell, Adele V., and George E. Peterson, eds. 1992. *Drugs, Crime, and Social Isolation: Barriers to Urban Opportunity.* Washington, DC: The Urban Institute.

Harré, H. Rom. 1979. *Social Being: A Theory for Social Psychology.* Oxford: Blackwell.

Hartigan, John, Jr. 1999. *Racial Situations: Class Predicaments of Whiteness in Detroit.* Princeton, NJ: Princeton University Press.

Hayden, Dolores. 2002. *Redesigning the American Dream: The Future of Housing, Work, and Family Life.* New York: W. W. Norton.

Hine, Darlene, William Hine, and Stanley Harrold. 2012. *African Americans: A Concise History.* 4th ed. Boston: Pearson Education.

Hochschild, Arlie. 1997. *The Time Bind: When Work Becomes Home and Home Becomes Work.* New York: Metropolitan/Holt.

Hochschild, Arlie. 2016. *Strangers in Their Own Land: Anger and Mourning on the American Right.* New York: The New Press.

Hochschild, Jennifer L. 1995. *Facing Up to the American Dream: Race, Class, and the Soul of the Nation.* Princeton, NJ: Princeton University Press, 1995.

Hodson, Randy. 2001. *Dignity at Work.* New York: Cambridge University Press.

Holstein, James A., and Jaber F. Gubrium. 2000. *The Self We Live By: Narrative Identity in a Postmodern World.* New York: Oxford University Press.

Holzer, Harry. 1996. *What Employers Want: Job Prospects for Less-educated Workers.* New York: Russell Sage Foundation Press.

Holzer, Harry, Peter Edelman, and Paul Offner. 2006. *Reconnecting Disadvantaged Young Men.* Washington, DC: Urban Institute Press.

Hunter, Marcus Anthony, and Zandria F. Robinson. 2016. "The Sociology of Urban Black America." *Annual Review of Sociology* 42: 385–405.

Jargowsky, Paul A., and M. Bane. 1991. "Ghetto Poverty in the United States, 1970 to 1980." In *The Urban Underclass*, edited by Christopher Jencks and Paul E. Peterson, 235–273. Washington, DC: The Brookings Institution.

Jargowsky, Paul A. 1997. *Poverty and Place: Ghettos, Barrios, and the American City*. New York: Russell Sage Foundation.

Jencks, Christopher, and Paul Peterson, eds. 1991. *The Urban Underclass*. Washington, DC: The Brookings Institution.

Johnson, Heather Beth. 2014. *The American Dream and the Power of Wealth: Choosing Schools and Inheriting Inequality in the Land of Opportunity*. New York: Routledge.

Kalleberg, Arne L. 2011. *Good Jobs, Bad Jobs: The Rise of Polarized and Precarious Employment Systems in the United States, 1970s–2000s*. American Sociological Association Rose Series in Sociology. New York: Russell Sage Foundation.

Kanter, Rosabeth Moss. 1977. *Men and Women of the Corporation*. New York: Basic Books.

Kimmel, Michael. 1996. *Manhood in America: A Cultural History*. New York: The Free Press.

Kirschenman, Joleen, and Kathryn M. Neckerman. 1991. "'We'd Love to Hire Them, But . . .' In *The Urban Underclass*, edited by Christopher Jencks and Paul E. Peterson. Washington, DC: The Brookings Institution.

Kusmer, Kenneth, and Joe W. Trotter, eds. 2009. *African American Urban History since World War II*. Chicago: University of Chicago Press.

Leduff, Charlie. 2014. *Detroit: An American Autopsy*. New York: Penguin.

Lemann, Nicholas, 1991. *The Promised Land: The Great Black Migration and How It Changed America*. New York: Alfred A. Knopf.

Liebow, Eliot. 1967. *Tally's Corner: A Study of Negro Streetcorner Men*. Boston: Little, Brown.

Lindsey, Howard O'Dell. 1993. "Fields to Fords, Feds to Franchise: African American Empowerment in Inkster, Michigan." PhD dissertation, University of Michigan.

Levy, Francesca. 2010. "America's Most Livable Cities." *Forbes*, April 29. https://www.forbes.com/2010/04/29/cities-livable-pittsburgh-lifestyle-real-estate-top-ten-jobs-crime-income.html#893840d63467.

Lynd, Robert S., and Helen M. Lynd. 1929. *Middletown: A Study in Contemporary American Culture*. New York: Harcourt, Brace.

Marks, Carole. 1988. *Farewell—We're Good and Gone: The Great Black Migration*. Bloomington: Indiana University Press.

Markus, Hazel Rose, and Paula Nurius. 1986. "Possible Selves." *American Psychologist* 41, no. 9: 945–969.

Marsh, Aarica. 2016. "More Than Rust: The Story of Ypsilanti." *Michigan Daily*, April 5. https://www.michigandaily.com/section/statement/more-rust.

Marshall, Alfred P. 1993. *Unconquered Souls: The History of the African American in Ypsilanti*. Ypsilanti, MI: Marlan Publishers.

Massey, Douglas S., and Nancy Denton. 1993. *American Apartheid: Segregation and the Making of the Underclass*. Cambridge, MA: Harvard University Press.

Mauer, Marc. 1996. *Race to Incarcerate*. New York: The New Press.

Milkman, Ruth. 1997. *Farewell to the Factory: Auto Workers in the Late Twentieth Century*. Berkeley: University of California Press.

Mincy, Ronald, ed. 2006. *Black Males Left Behind*. Washington, DC: Urban Institute Press.

Moen, Phyllis. 1992. *Women's Two Roles: A Contemporary Dilemma*. Santa Barbara, CA: Praeger.

Moen, Phyllis, and Patricia Roehling. 2005. *The Career Mystique: Cracks in the American Dream*. Lanham, MD: Rowman & Littlefield.

Moore, Doug. 2006. "In East St. Louis, Almost All the News Is Bad: Murder, Vote Fraud Overshadow a Proud Past." *The Record* (Bergen County, NJ), October 4, A17.

Moss, Philip, and Chris Tilly. 2001. *Stories Employers Tell: Race, Skill, and Hiring in America*. New York: Russell Sage Foundation Press.

Muirhead, Russell. 2007. *Just Work*. Cambridge, MA: Harvard University Press.

Murphy, Alexandra. Forthcoming. *When the Sidewalks End: Poverty and Isolation in an American Suburb*. New York: Oxford University Press.

NeighborhoodScout. 2016. www.neighborhoodscout.com.

Nelson, Margaret K., and Joan Smith. 1999. *Working Hard and Making Do: Surviving in Small Town America*. Berkeley and Los Angeles: University of California Press.

Newman, Katherine S. 2000. *No Shame in My Game: The Working Poor in the Inner City*. New York: Vintage.

Norman, Jon R. 2013. *Small Cities USA: Growth, Diversity, and Inequality*. New Brunswick, NJ: Rutgers University Press.

O'Connor, Carla. 1997. "Dispositions toward (Collective) Struggle and Educational Resilience in the Inner City: A Case Analysis of Six African-American High School Students." *American Educational Research Journal* 34, no. 4 (Winter): 593–629.

Oyserman, D., D. Bybee, K. Terry, and T. Hart-Johnson. 2004. "Possible Selves as Roadmaps." *Journal of Research in Personality* 38: 130–149.

Pager, Devah. 2007. *Marked: Race, Crime, and Finding Work in an Era of Mass Incarceration*. Chicago: University of Chicago Press.

Parker, Kim. 2015. "Women More Than Men Adjust Their Careers for Family Life." Pew Research Center, Facttank: Inside the Numbers. https://www.pewresearch.org/fact-tank/2015/10/01/women-more-than-men-adjust-their-careers-for-family-life/.

Pattillo, Mary. 1999. *Black Picket Fences: Privilege and Peril among the Black Middle Class*. Chicago: University of Chicago Press.

Pattillo, Mary. 2007. *Black on the Block: The Politics of Race and Class in the City*. Chicago: University of Chicago Press.

Perry-Jenkins, Maureen. 2005. "Work in the Working-Class: Challenges Facing Families." In *Work, Family, Health, and Well-Being*, edited by Suzanne Bianchi, Lynne Casper, and Rosalind King, 453–472. Mahwah, NJ: Lawrence Erlbaum Associates.

Peters, Jeremy M. 2005. "Auctioning Memories in a Town Haunted by the Klan." *New York Times*, May 23. https://www.nytimes.com/2005/05/23/us/auctioning-memories-in-a-town-haunted-by-the-klan.html.

Peterson, Sarah Jo. 2002. "The Politics of Land Use and Housing in World War II Michigan: Building Bombers and Communities." PhD dissertation/thesis, Yale University, New Haven, CT.

Pew Research Center. 2015. *Raising Kids and Running a Household: How Working Parents Share the Load*. https://www.pewsocialtrends.org/2015/11/04/raising-kids-and-running-a-household-how-working-parents-share-the-load/.

Pew Research Center. 2016. *On Views of Race and Inequality, Blacks and Whites Are Worlds Apart*. June 27. https://www.pewsocialtrends.org/2016/06/27/on-views-of-race-and-inequality-blacks-and-whites-are-worlds-apart/.

Putnam, Robert D. 2007. "Diversity and Community in the 21st Century: The 2006 Johan Skytte Prize Lecture." *Scandinavian Political Studies* 30, no. 2: 137–174.

Putnam, Robert. 2015. *Our Kids: The American Dream in Crisis.* New York: Simon & Schuster.

Raley, Sarah B., Marybeth J. Mattingly, and Suzanne M. Bianchi. 2006. "How Dual Are Dual Income Couples? Documenting Change from 1970 to 2001." *Journal of Marriage and the Family* 68: 11–28.

Rotundo, A. 1993. *American Manhood: Transformations in Masculinity from the Revolution to the Modern Era.* New York: Basic Books.

Sandberg, Sheryl. 2013. *Lean In: Women, Work, and the Will to Lead.* New York: Alfred A. Knopf.

Sayer, Liana. 2005. "Gender, Time and Inequality: Trends in Women's and Men's Paid Work and Free Time." *Social Forces* 84, no. 1: 285–303.

Schrock, Douglas, and Michael Schwalbe. 2009. "Men, Masculinity, and Manhood Acts." *Annual Review of Sociology* 35, no. 1: 277–295.

Schweinhart, Lawrence J. 2004. *The High/Scope Perry Preschool Study through Age 40.* Ypsilanti, MI: High/Scope Educational Research Foundation.

Schweinhart, Lawrence J., and D. Weikart. 1997. *Lasting Differences: The High/Scope Preschool Curriculum Comparison Study through Age 23.* Ypsilanti, MI: High/Scope Press.

Seelye, Katharine Q. 2011. "Detroit Census Figures Confirm a Desertion Like No Other." *New York Times* (New York ed.), March 23, A1.

SEMCOG (Southeast Michigan Council of Governments). 2006. ACS Data. www.city-data.com/city/.

SEMCOG (Southeast Michigan Council of Governments). 2010. ACS Data. www.city-data.com/city/.

Sharkey, Patrick. 2013. *Stuck in Place: Urban Neighborhoods and the End of Progress toward Racial Equality.* Chicago: University of Chicago Press.

Silva, Jennifer M. 2013. *Coming Up Short: Working-Class Adulthood in an Age of Uncertainty.* New York: Oxford University Press.

Simon, Darran. 2012. "With 59 Homicides in 2012, Camden Crosses a Grim Milestone." *The Philadelphia Inquirer*, November 17, A01.

Simpson, Ruth, Jason Hughes, and Natasha Slutskaya. 2016. *Gender, Class and Occupation: White Working Class Men Doing Dirty Work.* New York: Springer.

Slaughter, Anne-Marie. 2016. *Unfinished Business: Women, Men, Work, Family.* New York: Random House.

Sloane, Julie, and Tom Monaghan. 2003. "Tom Monaghan Domino's Pizza." *CNNMoney*, September 1. http://money.cnn.com/magazines/fsb/fsb_archive/2003/09/01/350799/.

Smock, Pamela J., and Mary Noonan. 2005. "Gender, Work, and Family Well-being in the United States." In *Work, Family, Health, and Well-Being*, edited by Suzanne Bianchi, Lynne Casper, and Rosalind King, 343–360. Mahwah, NJ: Lawrence Erlbaum Associates.

St. Jean, Yanick, and Joe R. Feagan. 1997. *Double Burden: Black Women and Everyday Racism.* New York: Routledge.

Stack, Carol B. 1975. *All Our Kin: Strategies for Survival in a Black Community.* New York: Harper & Row.

Stets, Jan E., and Michael J. Carter. 2011. "Understanding the Moral Self: Applying Identity Theory." *Social Psychology Quarterly* 74: 192–215.

Sugrue, Thomas, J. 1996. *The Origins of the Urban Crisis: Race and Inequality in Postwar Detroit.* Princeton, NJ: Princeton University Press.

Sullivan, Mercer. 1989. *Getting Paid: Youth, Crime and Work in the Inner City*. Ithaca, NY: Cornell University Press.

Sweet, Stephen, and Peter Meiksins. 2013. *Changing Contours of Work: Jobs and Opportunities in the New Economy*. 2nd ed. Sociology for a New Century Series. Thousand Oaks, CA: Pine Forge Press. (1st ed. 2008).

Taylor, Robert. J., and Sheril Sellers. 1997. "Informal Ties and Employment among Black Americans." In *Family Life in Black America*, edited by Robert J. Taylor, James S. Jackson, and Linda M. Chatters. Newbury Park, CA: Sage Publishers.

Tolnay, Stewart E. 2003. "The African American 'Great Migration' and Beyond." *Annual Review of Sociology* 29: 209–232.

Townsend, Nicholas. 2002. *Package Deal: Marriage, Work and Fatherhood in Men's Lives*. Philadelphia: Temple University Press.

Trotter, Joe William, ed. 1991. *The Great Migration in Historical Perspective: New Dimensions of Race, Class, and Gender*. Bloomington: Indiana University Press.

US Census Bureau. 1990. 1990 Census of Population: Social and Economic Characteristics, Michigan. US Department of Commerce Economics and Statistics Administration. https://www.census.gov/population/www/censusdata/90pubs/cp-2.html.

US Census Bureau. 2000a. Census 2000, Population and Housing Summary File 1. https://www.census.gov/census2000/sumfile1.html.

US Census Bureau. 2000b. American Community Survey (ACS). http://censtats.census.gov/data/MI/0602616189160.pdf.

US Census Bureau. 2000c. Profile of Selected Economic Characteristics: 2000, Census 2000 Summary File 3 (SF 3)—Sample Data. https://www.census.gov/census2000/sumfile3.html.

US Census Bureau. 2003. http://www.census.gov/acs/Products/Profiles/Single/2003/ACS/Narrative/050/NP05000US26161.htm.

US Census Bureau. 2006–2010. American Community Survey 5-Year Estimates. https://factfinder.census.gov/faces/tableservices/jsf/pages/productview.xhtml?src=bkmk.

US Census Bureau. 2010. Census 2010, Population and Housing Summary File 1. https://www.census.gov/prod/cen2010/doc/sf1.pdf.

US Census Bureau and Social Explorer. 1990. Social Explorer Tables (SE), Comprehensive Demographic Reports. https://www.socialexplorer.com/tables/C1990.

US Census Bureau and Social Explorer. 2000. Social Explorer Tables (SE), Comprehensive Demographic Reports. https://www.socialexplorer.com/tables/C2000.

US Census Bureau and Social Explorer. 2013. Social Explorer Tables: ACS 2013 (3-Year Estimates) (SE), ACS 2013 (3-Year Estimates). https://www.socialexplorer.com/data/ACS2013_3yr/metadata/.

Venkatesh, Sudhir. 2000. *American Project: The Rise and Fall of a Modern Ghetto*. Cambridge, MA: Harvard University Press.

Venkatesh, Sudhir. 2006. *Off the Books: The Underground Economy of the Urban Poor*. Cambridge, MA: Harvard University Press.

Wacquant, Loic. 2003. *Body and Soul: Notebooks of an Apprentice Boxer*. New York: Oxford University Press.

Wang, Wendy, Kim Parker, and Paul Taylor. 2013. *Breadwinner Moms*. Washington, DC: Pew Research Center. https://www.pewsocialtrends.org/2013/05/29/breadwinner-moms/.

Wiese, Andrew. 2004. *Places of Their Own: African American Suburbanization in the Twentieth Century*. Chicago: University of Chicago Press.

Williams, Joan. 1999. *Unbending Gender: Why Family and Work Conflict and What to Do about It*. New York: Oxford University Press.

Williams, Joan. 2010. *Reshaping the Work-Family Debate: Why Men and Class Matter*. Cambridge, MA: Harvard University Press.

Wilson, Marion F. 1956. *The Story of Willow Run*. Ann Arbor: University of Michigan Press.

Wilson, William Julius. 1987. *The Truly Disadvantaged: The Inner City, The Underclass, and Public Policy*. Chicago: University of Chicago Press.

Wilson, William Julius. 1996. *When Work Disappears: The World of the New Urban Poor*. New York: Alfred A. Knopf.

Yamiche, Alcindor. 2013. "Bloody Camden: This Isn't Newtown." *USA Today*, June 5, 1A.

Young, Alford A., Jr. 1999. "The (Non) Accumulation of Capital: Explicating the Relationship of Structure and Agency in the Lives of Poor Black Men." *Sociological Theory* 17, no. 2 (July): 201–227.

Young, Alford A., Jr. 2000. "On the Outside Looking In: Low-Income Black Men's Conceptions of Work Opportunity and the 'Good Job.'" In *Coping with Poverty: The Social Contexts of Neighborhood, Work, and Family in the African American Community*, edited by Sheldon Danziger and Ann Chin Lin, 141–171. Ann Arbor: University of Michigan Press.

Young, Alford A., Jr. 2004. *The Minds of Marginalized Black Men: Making Sense of Mobility, Opportunity, and Future Life Chances*. Princeton, NJ: Princeton University Press.

Young, Alford A., Jr. 2006. "Low-Income Black Men on Work Opportunity, Work Resources, and Job Training Programs." In *Black Males Left Behind*, edited by Ronald Mincy, 147–184. Washington, DC: Urban Institute Press.

Young, Alford A., Jr. 2008. "The Work-Family Divide for Low-Income African Americans." In *The Changing Landscape of Work and Family in the American Middle Class: Reports from the Field*, edited by Elizabeth Rudd and Lara Descartes, 87–115. Lanham, MD: Lexington.

Young, Alford A., Jr. 2010. "New Life for an Old Concept: Frame Analysis and the Reinvigoration of Studies in Culture and Poverty." In "Reconsidering Culture and Poverty," edited by Michele Lamont, Mario Small, and David Harding, issue of *Annals of the American Academy of Political and Social Science* 629 (May): 53–74.

Young, Alford A., Jr. 2013. "Uncovering a Hidden 'I' in Contemporary Urban Ethnography." *Sociological Quarterly* 51, no. 4: 51–65.

Young, Alford A., Jr. 2018. *Are Black Men Doomed?* London: Polity Press.

Ypsilanti, Michigan, Population. 2019. March 30. http://worldpopulationreview.com/countries/united-states-population/.

Zernike, Kate. 2014. "Camden Turns around with New Police Force." *New York Times*, September 1, sec. 1.

Index

affirmative action, 147
African American culture, 21, 23;
    poverty, 2; small city experience, 2,
    9; urban experience, 2
African Methodist Episcopal Society,
    25
agency, 9, 128, 129
Albion, Michigan, 51
American creed on upward mobility,
    67
American dream, 67
Anderson, Elijah, 153–154, 160n1, 167
Ann Arbor, 4, 5, 6, 7, 16, 17, 26, 35, 59,
    60–62, 73, 85, 98, 166
Appalachian region, 27

B-24 bombers, 26
Belleville, Michigan, 85
Bergmann, Luke, 43n3; *Getting Ghost*,
    43n3
black men, public identity, 154–155,
    157–158, 170; perceptions of,
    156–159
black women, perceptions of, 52
Blue Cross Blue Shield, 65

capital, forms of, 122, 125
chocolate cities, 18
Chicago, 21, 23, 97, 168
Chrysler Corporation, 26
Civil War, 26
Clum, Kimberly, 44n14
community studies, 167
concentration effects, 66–67
conspiracy theories, 148
crime, experiences with, 50, 55, 57,
    95–96
criminal records, 152; black men and,
    152–153

culture, street and decent, 153–154,
    160n1

Detroit, 3, 4, 5, 6, 17, 18, 19, 62–65, 73,
    168
Domino's Pizza, 27, 28
drug addiction, 50

Eastern Michigan University, 19, 100n2
education, 77, 86, 139, 143, 144, 147, 151
ESPN, 117
ethnography, 171n2; ethnographic
    interviewing, 8, 18, 100n3, 124–125

factories, 74, 74–75, 76, 83, 85, 113, 114,
    138, 164
fast food industry, 76–77, 77, 99n1;
    Burger King, 76; McDonald's, 76, 77,
    116
Federal Public Housing Commission,
    43n5
Ford, Henry, 25
Ford Motor Company, 26, 43n5, 50, 57,
    75, 82, 113; Visteon plant, 161;
    Willow Run Plant, 25, 26
functional selves, 122–123

General Motors Corporation, 16, 26
ghetto, 6; institutional ghetto, 23, 43n4
good jobs, 6, 8, 17, 82, 84, 145–146; and
    gender, 110–118, 119; qualities of,
    86–88, 129, 130, 153
green economy, 169

Hartigan, John, 43n3; *Racial Situations*,
    43n3
Head Start, 27–28
Huron River, 25

imagination, 8, 9, 83, 168

CPSIA information can be obtained
at www.ICGtesting.com
Printed in the USA
BVHW030313011019
559845BV00004B/5/P